The Acquisitive Distributor

4 KEYS TO SUCCESS WHEN BUYING A WHOLESALE DISTRIBUTION BUSINESS

BRENT R. GROVER

N·A·W
DREF
DISTRIBUTION RESEARCH AND
EDUCATION FOUNDATION

ISBN 0-9714752-0-2

Book design by Curry Graphics - www.carolcurry.com

Edited by Greg Erickson, NAW Director - Communications

TABLE OF CONTENTS

ABOUT THE AUTHOR

BRENT R. GROVER is a 25-year distribution industry
veteran, consultant, writer, CPA, and educator.
He can be reached at his firm, Evergreen Consulting, LLC
(brentgrover@evergreenconsultingllc.com).

Also by Brent R. Grover:

More to the Bottom Line:
Customer Profitability Tools for Distributors

ABOUT NAW

The National Association of Wholesaler-Distributors was created in 1946 to deal with issues of interest to the entire merchant wholesale distribution industry, thereby freeing affiliated associations to concentrate on the concerns specific to their commodity lines. NAW is a federation of 92 wholesale distribution line of trade national associations and thousands of individual firms which collectively total more than 40,000 companies. In addition to these corporate members and national associations, NAW lists several dozen state and regional groups on its comprehensive roster. The role of DREF within NAW is to sponsor and disseminate research into strategic management issues affecting the wholesale distribution industry.

NAW/DREF
1725 K. St., NW, Ste. 300
Washington, DC 20006
202-872-0885
www.naw.org

DEDICATION

This work is dedicated to those who volunteer their time to help others, especially the men and women who devote precious hours and energy to their trade associations.

Our chosen livelihood, the leadership and management of distribution companies, is enriched by the presence of strong, professional competitors. Trade associations bring us the relationships, information, and education needed to ensure our continued success.

B.R.G.

ACKNOWLEDGEMENTS

Thanks to NAW's Distribution Research and Education Foundation (DREF) Board for its willingness to take on this project. I'm grateful that DREF is willing to explore the edges of the art and science of distribution. While it's tempting to stay safely in the middle of the research spectrum, DREF's leadership is willing to gamble with the more fascinating possibilities.

Thanks to Andy Gelfand of Bruml Capital for his advice. Thanks also to my friend and colleague of many years, Dick Childers of The Childers Group.

I'm also indebted to my friends in the distribution trade association world, particularly Bill Frohlich and John Buckley. I won't name anyone else, for fear of leaving anyone out. Thanks to each and every one of you for wise counsel and access to invaluable insights and information.

Much of this work was done in the presence of, and sometimes at the expense of, my wife Candy and our four children. Everyone pitched in, especially Charlie, who did research, and Rob, who analyzed some of the survey data. Jack and Carlton, our seventh-graders, were thoughtful and supportive. Candy is a patient organizer, proofreader, and cheerleader.

DREF BOARD OF DIRECTORS

FOREWORD

The distribution industry has been at or near the top of merger and acquisition activity for the past 10 years. There are indications that a high level of distribution M&A will continue for the foreseeable future. This book takes the first close look at distributor M&A in the United States during the years of industry consolidation and beyond. It asks, and answers, a number of extremely important questions:

What is so unusual about buying a distribution business? What are some of the special considerations when buying an owner-managed business? Most important, why do so many acquisitions of distributors fail to meet the buyers' expectations?

The research behind this book includes a study of hundreds of acquisitions of distributors by hundreds of acquirers. Brent Grover interviewed more than 50 acquisitive distributors, as well as advisors and other M&A experts. He had two basic objectives in mind: to find the best practices behind deals that work and to unveil the "worst" practices behind acquisitions that *don't* succeed.

Brent's journey led him to focus on four deal-making phases used by all acquirers: strategy, negotiation, due diligence, and integration. He has isolated the processes used in each of the four phases and pinpoints the specific steps that predict ultimate success or failure in acquiring owner-managed distribution businesses.

Here Brent Grover recommends the following acquisitions strategy for your distribution business:

- Become a "serial acquirer" by making a small acquisition every year, or as fast as your company can digest the cost and management effort needed. Continual acquirers who make small deals, he says, earn higher returns than those with fewer but larger deals. Small acquisitions that add only 5% to your sales can jumpstart your company's growth. A slow-growth distributor (for example, 3% per year) can accelerate its average growth rate to 8% per year with a series of small acquisitions. Sustained growth at 8% per year compounds to doubling the company size in about nine years.

- Avoid the temptation to go after a "Big-Bang" acquisition that could jeopardize your company. Don't bet more than 10% of your net worth on any one transaction.

- Build deals based on the fundamental way your company makes money. Stick to your passion and your skills.

- Last but not least, use customer profitability information as your guidepost for evaluating and integrating acquisitions.

There is no magic formula, nor only one best way to go about making acquisitions. Brent's intention in doing the research and writing this book is to help you grow your distribution business by better understanding how successful acquisitive distributors operate.

Develop your strategy, refine your best practices, and avoid costly pitfalls.

Byron E. Potter, *Chairman*
Distribution Research and Education Foundation
March 2005

PREFACE

I have been involved in many distribution acquisitions for public and private companies, both buying and selling, spanning 22 years and two different lines of trade.

I think Brent's work is an excellent "primer" for the distributor thinking of adopting acquisition as part of a growth strategy and a useful "reminder" to those of us who have been down the road many times.

Points for special emphasis in the work, based on my experience:

- *Evaluating the culture of the target company.* How does one go about doing this? What are the key clues to look for? Success of a distributor acquisition is not really in the numbers; it's in how the people are going to react to the culture, mindset, and operating philosophy the buyer brings to the new company. Given the speed at which distributor business happens, if you greatly disrupt the culture and unsettle the people, you'll lose a lot of business and goodwill.

- *The Integration tasks section.* Emphasis on communication methods, timing, and techniques is critical here. The best game plan, if it is not communicated clearly, in proper sequence, and with effect will undermine all the "numbers." Many introspective CEOs may be proud of the deal they negotiate but not fully think through how they should inform the seller's employees on the value of that deal. At the end of the day, almost everything about the deal, its timing, and overall terms will be known by everybody. Buyers have to decide whether they want to be viewed with credibility because they got the news out first, or with skepticism because the information came to key people from other sources.

- *The special issues section in Chapter Eight.* Many times the deal will be won or lost by how the buyer allows the owner to save face with family members, arrange for extension of lifestyle items, or come up with creative ways to handle issues like health insurance coverage. Building on a primary theme of the book, distributors are all about people—and the owner's family has to be attended to, whether they stay or not.

I agree with Brent's assessment that some 70% of deals either fail or don't live up to potential. I think it's a lack of people, leadership, and communication skills that sink more deals than an inability to correctly assess the numbers or strategy.

Mark W. Kramer, *CEO*
Laird Plastics
April 2005

INTRODUCTION

I was conflicted as I pulled my car out of the driveway on the sunny October morning our deal was supposed to close. I didn't know if I should turn right, to the lawyers' office downtown, or left, toward the Metropark. After months of negotiating, analyzing, and agonizing, did I really want to sell the family distribution business? Or would it be best to just take a long drive and enjoy the colorful Ohio fall foliage?

The proposal for the sale of our distribution business had literally washed over the transom. The deal process had started with a phone call nearly a year prior: a late afternoon drink, a breakfast, and then a meeting at the accountants' office one Saturday a few weeks later. Slowly at first, then more forcefully, we were asked to consider letting the buyer use our 85-year-old business as the platform for a new, national supplier destined to become a major player in our line of trade.

Like the shareholders of so many owner-managed distribution companies, we were accustomed to eating well. Our business was strong, with growing sales and high profit levels. There were no signs of an economic reversal on the horizon in early 1999.

However, while we were eating well, we were no longer sleeping quite as well as we used to. We were increasingly aware that most of our operating profits were coming from a small number of very large customers. As many distributors do, we also felt pressure from the credit risk of very large receivables. Some of our major customers were having trouble paying their bills on time, and we had already experienced a million-dollar plus credit loss from a failed customer.

Should we cash in our chips or stay in the game? So many of the owner-managed distributors in our line of trade had already sold. Would we become the last of a dying breed or, as one of our board members suggested, the last girl at the dance? What would it be like to become an employee of a larger organization? As the new company grew, would our team be part of the leadership team, or would we all go our separate ways?

As I pondered which way to turn—downtown or to the park—the CEO of the buyer company was undoubtedly on a cell phone in his hotel room. The closing of our transaction had been delayed for two days due to last-minute problems. He'd had to juggle his travel schedule and deal with his fellow executives, bankers, lawyers, and a representative from a private-equity firm. Everyone on his team was under pressure to close the deal and move on to another transaction that was also well underway.

Would the deal finally close today? Due to other commitments, many of the people had to leave by late afternoon, no matter what. Would another delay cause the transaction to fall apart?

My brother, who was also my partner in selling the company, had been called away on business. He had already signed the documents, which were still awaiting my signature. Were the papers, requiring hundreds of signoffs, in order? We were still haggling over a large customer payment, promised but not yet received. The bank had an incorrect account number on a wire transfer. We needed a signature from an employee who was out of town. What else would go wrong?

As a seller, little did I know that this was just an ordinary day in the life of an acquisitive distributor.

Most acquisitions don't meet the buyer's expectations

We resolved the remaining issues and the documents were finalized as the day wore on. The needed signatures were added and the wire transfers went through the banking system. The lawyers opened a bottle of champagne for the customary toasts and promises, and the out-of-towners headed for the airport.

The CEO of the company that bought our business was frazzled that day. He was under intense pressure, but not only from the myriad details needed to close our deal. He was in the midst of other transactions that needed his attention. Some were still in the exploratory stage, some were being negotiated, and still others were in due diligence. Our company was about to enter the integration process.

As distributor acquisitions go, our transaction had a high likelihood of meeting the buyer's expectations. The buyer had a well-defined strategy, the transaction was negotiated with care, and the due diligence was thorough. If the integration was handled right, we were likely to achieve our projected financial goals. Our company was a mature distribution business with a strong track record, capable and experienced employees, and a diverse list of attractive customers and suppliers.

Yet, more often than not, acquisitions fail to meet the buyers' expectations.

After working at a national accounting firm and teaching at a business school, I spent over 20 years as a manager, and 10 years as CEO of National Paper and Packaging Co., a well-regarded and successful distributor of paper, packaging, and sanitary supplies and equipment. Our sale of the 85-year old business to a private-equity firm was our first real experience in the high-stakes world of M&A.

I had a front-row seat to the consolidation in our corner of the distribution industry during my years at National. Many of our fellow National Paper Trade Association members sold their businesses to the major industry consolidators during my service to NPTA as a volunteer leader, including chairman (1993). After their sales, my friends left their companies (voluntarily or otherwise) in the hands of new management. All too often, the acquired company rapidly lost many of its top-performing employees and most profitable customers.

Buyers sometimes found unpleasant surprises that might have been discovered before closing had the due diligence been performed properly. Others handled the integration of the acquired business so badly that even a casual observer could have detected the seeds of disaster.

Some distributors perform quite well after being sold, and there are examples of stellar results. Unrealistic buyer expectations (expressed in terms of inflated purchase prices and excessive debt loads) have resulted in disappointments even in some cases of good operating results. The balance sheets of many acquirers have included massive amounts of goodwill (prices paid in excess of book value of assets acquired), ultimately written off against the net worth of the buyers. The question often raised: Do acquisitions increase or destroy shareholder value?

My survey results and interviews with hundreds of acquisitive distributors (see Statement of Methodology) show that many buyers get good results from their acquisitions programs because they do it right. They buy the right companies for the right reasons. They pay the right price, structure the deal the right way, and take on the right amount of debt. They perform their due diligence the right way. Most important, they integrate their acquisitions into their organization the right way.

During the past three years, Evergreen Consulting has advised numerous clients in the acquisitions of distributors. We have also facilitated the sale of distribution businesses. These transactions were in several different distribution lines of trade, and each involved owner-managed companies. Our discipline applied in the four phases of deal making (strategy, negotiation, due diligence, and implementation) has yielded excellent results so far.

Brent R. Grover
Chautauqua, New York
March 2005

STATEMENT OF METHODOLOGY

Survey

NAW sent an Internet-based survey form to CEOs of wholesaler-distributor member companies, targeting experienced distributor executives whose companies had been active in the acquisition of other distribution businesses.

My questionnaire went into great depth about merger and acquisition practices in the distribution industry, including formulation of acquisition strategy, negotiation and deal structuring, financial and business due diligence, and integration practices. Respondents were asked to provide details about their three largest acquisitions, as well as an assessment of their most successful and least successful deals. Additional questions were posed about deal process, including the use of outside advisors.

Over 450 completed questionnaires were processed along with the details of 185 acquisitions of distributors by other distributors. The survey resulted in what I believe to be the most extensive data ever collected about M&A in the distribution industry.

Interviews

Structured interviews were held with 66 distributor CEOs who volunteered through the survey process. My interviewers asked the CEOs to share stories about the lessons they learned from their acquisition experiences. The CEOs were also asked for advice they would give to an executive thinking of acquiring a distribution business.

Other sources

Traditional sources were used to gather information about public companies, such as MergerStat Review, Capital IQ, Robert Baird, and Fleet Capital. Some of the standard M&A texts were consulted, as well as popular business books including *Good to Great*. As always, *Harvard Business Review* articles were a rich source of timeless information and analysis. The archives of my favorite distribution-specific journal, *MDM (Modern Distribution Management)* provided much valuable material.

CHAPTER ONE

*Acquiring a Distributor Is Different
from Buying Other Types
of Businesses*

"The smarter you play, the luckier you'll be."

Mark Pilarski

• • • • • • • •

Buying a distributor is unlike purchasing most other types of businesses, for two reasons. First, the most important asset the buyer is going to receive is difficult to pin a value on. Second, the buyer will most likely be dealing with an owner-manager. This chapter will explore these two issues—one straightforward and financial; the other, somewhat more mysterious.

Generally, 80% of a distributor's assets are receivables and inventories. The other 20% are vehicles, warehouse, and office equipment. These assets are easy to identify, audit, and value. None of them, however, is the most important item in the transaction.

The acquirer is expecting to obtain the distributor's customer relationships. These are intangible, mostly undocumented. Much of the distributor's business is not in the form of long-term contracts. Even when contracts are used, the customer often has the ability to cancel.

The primary relationship between distributor and customer is usually a personal one. Sales representatives and sometimes other personnel from the distributor have longtime relationships with one or more of the customer decision makers. Evaluating the long-term security of these relationships is highly subjective; mistakes are potentially lethal.

The distributor employees who developed and maintain the customer connections are critical to the stability of the business relationship. Beware the distributor who does not have employment contracts, or at least strong, stable relationships, with its key employees.

Premium: paying more than book value

The premium value of a distribution business is the amount the buyer is willing to pay above the net book value (carrying value minus related liabilities) of the receivables, inventories, and equipment. The premium, or purchase price in excess of book value of the assets, is often referred to as goodwill.

Here is a brief accounting lesson, for those who need a refresher. Book value is the amount at which assets are carried on the distributor's balance sheet. Receivables are recorded at the invoice amounts billed to the customers, usually less a reserve for uncollectible invoices. Inventories are recorded at the amount paid for the products, with some variations such as a LIFO (last-in, first out) inventory reserve. Vehicles, warehouse, and office equipment are recorded at the original purchase price, less the cumulative amount written off as depreciation. An example of a related liability is accounts payable.

If a distributor were to sell its assets at book value, the buyer would hand over a check for that amount. The distributor would use the proceeds from the asset sale to pay off its debts, including payables owed to suppliers. The amount left over (before taxes) would be the net book value of the business.

Most prospective sellers aren't keen on the idea of selling their business at book value, but sometimes they are fortunate to get that much. A distribution business without a track record of healthy profits and good prospects for future profits may be unable to obtain any premium. Getting book value for the assets is much better than selling for liquidation value.

Liquidation value is the amount for which the individual assets would sell in an auction environment. For example, the vehicles and other equipment would rarely bring their depreciated value at a sheriff's sale. The inventories would typically be sold off at a substantial reduction from their original cost. Receivables owed to a liquidating company can be difficult to collect.

Financial experts have devised methods to assign a value to intangible assets such as customer lists (or patents and other intellectual property). The practical application of these tools was to enable buyers to allocate the purchase price to the assets received in an acquisition. An example is the Iowa Curve, a mathematical model used to predict the gradual loss of customers in future years. While these statistical methods are useful for tax accounting, they aren't used to appraise customer lists.

Buyers often pay much more than book value, and they sometimes pay less.

Customer profitability analysis

How much is a portfolio of customer relationships worth to a prospective buyer? How would an acquisition-minded company go about valuing the customers of a target company?

Customer profitability analysis (CPA) is a widely accepted management tool used by wholesaler-distributors to evaluate the profitability of individual customers and groups of customers.

Customer profitability information, in the form of customer P&L statements and ranking reports, is critical for identifying and protecting the small number of customers who generate most of the distributor's operating profits. Customer P&L statements also pinpoint the large customers that actually cost the distributor money so that corrective actions can be taken. Customer profitability ranking reports are used to segment customers based on profit potential, to identify customers for additional investment, and to develop sales policies to optimize long-term profits. CPA information is also used for strategy development as well as for tactical purposes. See my DREF book *More to the Bottom Line: Customer Profitability Tools for Wholesale Distributors* (www.nawpubs.org) for a comprehensive review of CPA.

Customer profitability audits are an invaluable tool for ongoing distributor management as well as an indispensable aid for evaluating acquisition targets.

Customer profitability analysis is also a powerful way for the acquisitive company to value a target company's customer relationships. CPA can be used in the due diligence process to evaluate the prospective acquisition and to validate the assumptions in the acquisition model.

Future cash flows from a distributor's customer relationships are the earning power the buyer expects from the business. The buyer's challenge is to project the stability of those relationships.

Most distribution businesses are owner-managed

A large percentage of U.S. wholesaler-distributors are privately held businesses. This means, of course, that the acquisitive company will most often be targeting businesses managed by the owner or a member of the family that owns the company. The owner-managed business scenario presents some special challenges and sensitivities not seen when dealing with executives of large, professionally managed public companies.

Look at the business world through the owner-manager's glasses

The business world looks different to the CEO (chief executive *owner*, in this case) of an owner-managed company. The differences can be understood best by looking through his or her glasses. Some of the key issues can be described by examples.

The CEO of an owner-managed distribution company has a very fuzzy boundary between business life and personal life. His obligations to the company and to the family are mixed together. The CEO may deal with parents and children at work, as well as other family members including aunts, uncles, and cousins. The business is ever-present at home for the same reasons. The owner-manager CEO is seen as the leader of the business and possibly the leader of the family. In many cases the CEO is also expected to be a community leader, serving on the board of a local hospital or college, United Way, etc. These obligations leave little time for anything else. The CEO is a hard person to reach and is often very distracted.

The third-generation owner (3GO) is a grandchild of the founder. This is an individual who has been in or around the business throughout life. Often well-educated, perhaps with an advanced degree in business or law, the 3GO may have gained some work experience outside the family's business. The 3GO may have been raised with the clear expectation of being a future leader of the family enterprise. There are powerful emotional ties to the business, as well as burdens, that come with being a 3GO.

The conscientious owner-manager distribution CEO faces another set of obligations that necessitate a large amount of time away from the office. Due to the supplier-driven nature of distribution, the CEO is called away to meetings with suppliers. Frequent business trips to supplier councils, training meetings, strategy meetings, buying/marketing group meetings, and trade association meetings place further time pressures on the CEO.

The CEO of the target owner-managed company is under severe time pressure. This individual does not generally welcome calls or letters from prospective suitors. And, unlike CEO counterparts in the world of public companies, the owner-manager CEO does not necessarily have a duty to report such inquiries to an outside board of directors.

Getting the owner-manager CEO to focus on your proposition may be like dealing with someone who has a form of attention-deficit disorder. Your voice messages may go unanswered, your e-mails may be erased or eaten by the spam filter, and your letters may be tossed unopened into the wastebasket. That doesn't mean the CEO isn't interested. You just aren't getting through to him.

Take a walk in the owner-manager's shoes

Remember the scene in the wonderful movie *To Kill A Mockingbird*, in which Atticus Finch (Gregory Peck) taught his young daughter Scout to take a walk in the other person's shoes? I am asking you to consider walking in the shoes of the distributor owner-manager.

The owner-manager is often isolated in several ways. There may be a layer of insulation (employees) between the CEO and the company's trading partners, its customers, and suppliers. There may also be some protective padding (other managers) between the CEO and many of the company's employees. Due to the demands of a heavy travel schedule and outside commitments, much of what the CEO knows about the business is filtered. Staff sometimes removes bad news from the information flow before it reaches the CEO. Supplier executives tend to use happy talk when meeting with distributor CEOs. Many of the distributor CEO's meetings with customers are prearranged feel-good sessions with large, satisfied loyalists. The owner-manager CEO is, therefore, isolated. He is aware of it and doesn't like it, but has no time to do anything much about it.

Family pressures attack the owner-manager CEO from several angles. The business provides a lifestyle to a group of family stakeholders, some of whom may no longer work at the company (or possibly never did). The business pays salaries to those who are on the payroll, retirement benefits to those who are no longer on the payroll, rent to those who are landlords, and interest payments to those who provide capital and dividends to those who own shares. There may be a preceding generation that wants to have a voice in the company's affairs and a succeeding generation that wishes to have a say as well. The beleaguered CEO is the arbiter of all disputes and the one who must settle all grievances, real or imagined.

Like all CEOs, the owner-manager must face the cash-flow demands of the business, the competition for scarce resources of time and capital, and the demands of key employees, whether family or non-family. In a smaller company there may be a lack of staff with special skills in areas such as finance, human resources, marketing, information systems, and logistics. The CEO may have to serve as the ultimate resource in solving complex problems or find someone outside the company who can.

Finally, the owner-manager CEO must confront some special brands of fear. There are, of course, things all CEOs are afraid of, such as running out of cash or losing a major customer or supplier. In addition, there is the worry of not having a qualified successor. Who will take over on an interim (or permanent) basis if the CEO is suddenly unable to serve due to health problems or other reasons? Will the employees, customers, suppliers, lenders, and other owners support the successor, or will there be a bloody coup?

Another common fear of owner-manager CEOs is lack of an exit strategy. There is much common wisdom, such as the "third generation jinx," that discourages the idea of passing the business on to another generation of family owner-management. Some CEOs have competent children who do not want to come into the business; others have less competent children who do. The business may have trouble attracting or holding on to qualified non-family people who feel they will never have a chance to run the company or fear working for the next generation. Unfortunately, some owner-managers with great businesses either feel immortal or just don't take the time to devise a workable succession plan. They may awaken one day and realize that it's too late to repair the damage done by years of neglect.

What does this mean to the would-be acquirer of such a business? By taking the time to study and understand the position that the target company's CEO is in, the prospective acquirer may find ways that an acquisition can resolve many of these problems. It's no fun to be isolated, overworked, overwhelmed, pressured, and afraid. The proposed acquisition must make sense to both buyer and seller in terms of the financial issues, of course. But to get the attention and support of the owner-manager CEO, it is helpful to walk a mile or two in his shoes.

CHAPTER TWO

*Recent History of
Distributor Acquisitions*

"Nobody is always a winner, and anybody who says he is, is either a liar or doesn't play poker."

"Amarillo Slim" Preston
• • • • • • • • • • • • •

Japanese distributors have a dramatically different view of acquisitions than their counterparts in North America. I was invited to the Bellagio hotel in Las Vegas in 2002 to present a two-day briefing about mergers and acquisitions to 32 top executives from leading Japanese distributors. I was shocked to find that three of the companies had been in the hands of the same family for 12 or more generations—300 years or more. The two or three largest companies had revenues in the $300–$500 million range, but the typical firm was small: $25 million in sales and only one or two locations. Mergers were almost unheard of. Why?

The tradition of family ownership was so strong that most of the distributor owner-managers would not have considered selling their company under any circumstances. Selling out might have been considered a victory of one family over another. Sale of an enterprise handed down from generation to generation was thought by many to be a betrayal of their ancestors. Some of the executives were groomed for their family company leadership position almost from the day they were born. Would it be better to liquidate a failing business rather than turn it over to another family?

In contrast, mergers and acquisitions among American distributors have become so common that news of most transactions no longer raises eyebrows.

Distributor consolidation circa 1980–2000

Some experts have long predicted the demise of small distribution businesses in the United States. Magazine articles and even some books have been devoted to the subject. It's been said that only large companies compete effectively due to economies of scale, meet the demands of national customers, fulfill the needs of huge suppliers, etc. Small distributors were advised to get big, get specialized, or get out. The specialization route has led some distributors to become "boutique" distributors, offering niche services that others couldn't provide profitably or just weren't interested in. Myriad other factors have contributed to the explosion of M&A activity.

Why so many owner-managed businesses sold

Many distributor owners started their business careers after World War II and reached retirement age in the 1980s and 1990s. They looked around and did not have a qualified/interested family member available to continue family ownership of the business. The educational opportunities available to family members enabled them to become highly paid professionals or enter other fields rather than go directly into the family business. Many never seriously considered joining the family enterprise. The increased mobility in American society scattered families about the country for higher education and jobs in other cities. Many of the potential successors never returned home to the business.

The threat of estate and gift taxes posed a potential liquidity crisis for many family businesses. Attorneys and accountants advised their clients to sell the company rather than leave their heirs the challenge of financing estate tax obligations out of cash flow.

Buyers competed vigorously for good distribution businesses, offering prices and terms that many sellers found impossible to resist. They were able to secure their financial future and provide for their heirs by selling their companies years earlier than they would have considered possible.

Constantly changing tax laws tended to move in favor of selling small businesses. Reductions in capital gains rates and creative tax ideas made it possible for sellers to reduce, postpone, or even avoid some federal and state income taxes. Strong investment markets provided returns that made a sale even more compelling.

Employment-related litigation, product liability risks, the quality movement, and the need to make large investments in new technologies made running even a small distribution business more and more complex. The explosion of information, the need for speed-based competition, and the demands of customers and suppliers overwhelmed some owners.

Naturally, many companies went up for sale for reasons such as the poor health or death of an owner, cash-flow problems, or simply an owner's desire to retire in style and fulfill his fantasies (or at least some of them).

High prices

An overarching reason why so many owner-managed distributors changed hands during the consolidation phase is the high prices paid by buyers. The rumor mill among distributor owners overflowed with questions like, "Did you hear how much so-and-so got for his business?" Many of the rumors were false, but the prices paid did reach levels that prospective sellers never dreamed of. Owners called in M&A experts to place a value on their businesses for estate-planning purposes or otherwise and were often pleasantly surprised. The advisors' valuations—realistic or not—often started a process that led to the sale of the business.

The best distribution businesses were targeted by the consolidators and subjected to a courtship process that sometimes was initiated at trade association meetings or other industry gatherings. Those distributors who were fortunate enough to be among the most successful in their geographic areas were the most inviting targets for the consolidators. A large, profitable wholesaler-distributor presented the best opportunity to gain market share quickly. Many buyers avoided turnaround situations due to a shortage of capable managers to step in to fix the problems. In some cases bidding wars erupted and lucky sellers were able to pit consolidators against one another to elevate prices even further.

Deal structure

The buyer's stock was used as currency in many deals, even though most sellers traditionally preferred the security of cash. The use of the buyer's stock can be advantageous to both buyer and seller: The buyer is able to conserve cash, of course, and (in the past) could enjoy a favorable accounting method known as "pooling of interests."

When stock is received instead of cash, the seller is able to postpone paying income taxes on the gain until the eventual sale of the shares received in the transaction. On the negative side, the seller is often required to hold on to the shares received for a long period of time (although there are ways to limit some of the risk). For some, holding the buyer's stock was a windfall; for others, a disaster.

Typically, accountants and lawyers advise their clients to sell their stock rather than the company's assets. One reason is to avoid higher income taxes. Depending on the company's tax circumstances, the company pays income tax on its gain on the sale of its assets; then the shareholders pay income tax on their gain when the cash is distributed to them.

Most buyers strongly prefer to purchase the assets from the seller's corporation for at least two reasons. When assets are purchased, the buyer may be able to allocate some of the purchase price to assets eligible for a fast tax write-off. The tax advantages of this compared to buying the seller's stock can be significant. Avoiding risk of exposure to the corporation's liabilities is even more important to many buyers. Purchasing the sellers' stock may subject the new owner to unrecorded liabilities of the corporation, such as employment practices claims, product liability claims, taxes resulting from tax audits, benefit plan liabilities, and others. Warranties and representations from the seller may provide some protection for the buyer, but the buyer is generally better off purchasing the corporation's assets rather than its stock.

The strong sellers' market for wholesale distribution businesses enabled many sellers to get not only the price but also the terms they wanted. Buyers were tempted to purchase stock even though they ordinarily would have refused to do so. Many buyers were flexible, willing to pay cash or provide generous amounts of their stock to sellers willing to take the additional risk (and enjoy the prospective benefits).

Distribution company transactions were among the 10 most active M&A industry categories, in terms of number of transactions, during the 1990–2000 period. But distributor M&A deal activity dropped off suddenly when the bottom fell out of the acquisitions market. Is the consolidation era over? Industry observers predict that consolidation will continue in the distribution field. Will the deal-making activity again reach the feverish pace of the first phase of consolidation?

I feel that the next phase of consolidation won't be another feeding frenzy. The driving force of at least some of the deal-making passion was the high prices being paid for wholesaler-distributors. Some owner-managers accelerated their long-term plans for a "liquidity event" when they felt they should grab the money while it was still on the table. Strategic buyers took many attractive distribution companies off the market. Many distribution industries now have two or three major players who have succeeded in filling in their strategic map of locations throughout the company. It is hard to imagine that there will be a repetition of the bidding wars where two major buyers go after the same strategic target.

Rollups, roll-outs, and private-equity deals

The "IPO roll-out" concept for distributors has taken on a bad name following the some of the notable failures. Private-equity firms are likely to be more cautious in their valuations of wholesale distribution firms, due to the poor track record of many distributor deals. The sophisticated institutional investors behind large private-equity funds are more demanding today, due to changes in the investing climate.

Recent disclosures about private-equity fund performance (*The Economist*, December 2004) raise questions about uneven performance and very high management fees. CALPERS, a large retirement fund known for making private-equity investments, was forced to reveal the fees it has paid to private-equity funds, along with the investment results. The golden age of private-equity funds and the infusion of capital into buying distributors may be over, at least for now.

Strategic acquisitions by local and regional distributors

A good argument can be made for a flurry of acquisitions of distributors by other distributors. Those who remained independent through the first waves of consolidation and survived the shakeout in their industry may find their best growth option is acquiring other distributors. The purchases may be merely opportunistic, such as when a target company falls into their lap. Or they may choose to become an acquisitive distributor and follow a disciplined growth program.

Many large distributors grow much more from acquisitions than organically

The largest distribution firms typically have followed one of two paths to building their large organizations. One is the patient, long-term addition of "greenfield" locations with an occasional acquisition. An example of this approach is Applied Industrial Technologies (AIT, formerly Bearings Inc.). Over several decades, Bearings Inc. opened dozens of company-owned locations throughout much of the country. Large acquisitions (Dixie Bearings) were the exception. Historically, AIT achieved its strong position in the industry by growing organically through reinvestment of the company's earnings. More recently, AIT has accelerated its growth into new markets, products, and services through acquisitions. W.W. Grainger is another example of patient, organic growth over decades of reinvestment of profits in the business. By comparison, Genuine Parts, consisting of four large distribution divisions, added three of those businesses to its traditional automotive parts. One of its major acquisitions, Motion Industries, now makes up a significant portion of total corporate sales.

Some large distributors are primarily industry consolidations

Sysco is one of the great success stories in the wholesale distribution industry. After going public in 1970 with $115 million in sales, Sysco grew over 34 years to $26 billion in sales and paid 134 consecutive quarterly dividends to its shareholders.

Sysco got its humble start as a foodservice distribution rollup. Through a series of acquisitions, pursuant to a sound strategy and excellent integration, Sysco has been among the top performers among publicly held distributors for more than 20 years.

Most distributor rollups have not worked, no matter the line of trade

The idea behind what has become known as a stock rollup is fairly simple: Some distributor owners get together and form a new corporation. The individual owners exchange their ownership in their individual companies for stock in the new entity (and possibly some cash and debt). The new entity then has the critical mass to compete against the larger players in the line of trade. The former company owners, now shareholders in the new business, continue to operate their companies. With continued success, the rollup goes public and uses its rising stock value to attract even more companies. In time, the stock in the rollup becomes very valuable, and everybody wins. Unfortunately, most of the rollups haven't worked.

A prime example of a large-scale failure is an office supply and furnishings distribution rollup that started out in 1995. After forming a nucleus of companies, the business went public and enjoyed rapid growth in revenues due to acquisitions. By the end of 1996, the company had made 130 acquisitions and reached revenues of $3 billion.

Eventually the revenue growth from acquisitions slowed down, and the business went into a downward spiral. As revenue growth deteriorated, earnings fell and the stock dropped precipitously. The shareholders became worried and disillusioned. The company's inability to make further acquisitions with its deflated stock caused revenue growth to stop almost completely. Its leader, a man *Fortune* magazine once called the "wizard of deal-making," moved on to other projects in 1998, leaving the owner-managers in an unhappy situation.

An IPO rollup in the industrial supplies segment started with nine companies having combined sales of $251 million, The business raised $64 million when it went public in 1997. Industrial distribution may have seemed ripe for a rollup: There were a large number of small owner-managed distributors, many with limited capital and outdated systems, but facing growing demands from their high-tech manufacturing customers. The company eventually filed for bankruptcy.

Private-equity firms

Private-equity firms entered the distribution acquisition market with an optional way to finance a rollup. Instead of exchanging stock for an owner's interest in his distribution business, the private-equity firm is able to offer cash or a combination of cash and debt.

The typical private-equity firm has access to a large amount of cash from two sources: investors in its fund and lenders. The investors are often institutions such as large pension funds, endowments, and banks. The private-equity firm locates a small number of investors willing to make large commitments to a new fund. The fund size may be $100–500 million or more. Depending on the circumstances, such as the need to diversify risk, each fund may make 10 or more investments. For example, a $500 million fund may be interested in making 10 investments of $50 million each. Private-equity firms with strong track records can attract funds from the largest institutions and have the ability to obtain loans from the largest lenders. A major fund may be able to invest $50 million of equity in a particular deal and obtain loan commitments of $50 million or more for an attractive deal. With such a large checkbook, a private-equity fund can purchase very large wholesaler-distributors for cash.

Due to the amount of risk in private equity, large institutional investors anticipate premium returns on their investment, perhaps a 20%–30% annual return, with the expectation that they will get their money back in seven to 10 years. The private-equity firms are challenged to maintain a record of outstanding success in order to continue to attract investors to their new funds. The competition for the most attractive deals is intense. The fund managers often earn a 2% annual fee on the money they manage plus 20% of the fund's eventual profits.

In a possible scenario, a former executive from a large, nationally known distribution company approaches private firms with plans to do an "industry consolidation" in his former line of trade or some other. (The expression "industry consolidation" is more polite, since the term "rollup" is out of favor.) The executive is looking for a financial backer so he can play the role of promoter and founding CEO, using his industry knowledge and contacts to get the new company started. The promoter may put some of his own money into the deal, but his intention is to get a good-sized slice of the new business for himself and members of his team, usually a handful of the executive's former colleagues. The big money will come from a private-equity firm's investment fund. The business plan is usually shown to many private-equity firms before the executive is lucky enough—if he *is* lucky enough—to find an interested investor.

The promoter's acquisition strategy will have to be compelling and offer enough potential for growth in revenue, profits, and upside valuation to appeal to the institutional investors and prospective lenders. This proposition is a challenge for most distribution businesses. Investors cannot expect a windfall from putting their money into what is usually a slow-growth industry. Growth spurts in distribution almost always come through acquisitions. When the buyer runs out of good companies to acquire, targets available at a reasonable price, or cash, investors are quick to withdraw whatever capital they can and move on.

A large janitorial supplies roll-up is an example of distribution industry consolidation financed by a private-equity firm. The janitorial and sanitary supplies distributor is a portfolio company of GTCR Golder Rauner LLC, a large and well-established private-equity firm with over 150 acquisitions since 1980. The janitorial supplies distribution company was organized in 1997 and made 41 acquisitions within five years.

An industrial products distribution rollup was formed in June 1998 by a former president and CEO of a large office products supplier, in partnership with private-equity investor Wind Point Partners. The venture developed into a rollup of full-line industrial distributors, with an acquisition/consolidation strategy to build a $1 billion-plus hub-and-spoke industrial distribution company focusing on national contracts and integrated supply, as well as one-stop shopping for smaller accounts The company partnered with Wind Point in early 1998, with $250 million allocated for acquisitions, to fuel its growth plans in the then-heady environment for consolidation of industrial distribution companies.

Another major distributor Chapter 11 filing in this particular line of trade occurred in 1993, when the platform company, purchased by American Metals Industry Wholesalers in 1991, acquired several East Coast distributors and rolled them into a $45-million business. The company then filed Chapter 11 and six months later liquidated, leaving a trail of lawsuits and many owners who had sold their companies into the venture holding nothing but worthless stock.

Flawed acquisition strategy is often cited as a cause for failure

Tom Gale reported on the sad story of the end of another roll-up in *Modern Distribution Management*, June 2002:

> "The Chapter 7 bankruptcy filing by [the company], as reported in May 2002, was little more than a formality for a company that passed away in 2001. In reality, the 136-year-old company started into a freefall more than two years before the bankruptcy filing, and was ultimately a victim of the economy, consolidation, and the merger-and-acquisition mania of the 1990s.

> A source close to the situation observed many of the same factors that forced other distributor roll-ups into bankruptcy: an aggressive growth model based on acquisitions, difficulty integrating acquired companies, and investors from outside the industry. (Outsiders sometimes fail to understand the dynamics of connecting customers, distributors, and suppliers to generate a revenue stream.)

CHAPTER THREE

The Four Phases of an Acquisition

"One should always play fair when one has the winning cards."

Oscar Wilde
• • • • • • • •

Library and bookstore shelves are filled with books about mergers and acquisitions. They can be divided into two broad categories: "how-to" handbooks (*M&A for Dummies?*) and academic texts about M&A theory.

Striking a balance between the needs of business people who want to get straight to the point and those who need some backup information is a tricky act. It would be convenient to boil the entire subject down to a few bullet points, but oversimplification would scare away the skeptics. There are tons of research available to produce documentation for every point, but few would have the patience to read it.

To reach as many wholesale distribution executives as possible, and to be useful as well as thoughtful, each of the next four chapters is devoted to one of the four basic phases of the acquisition process:

1. Strategy
2. Negotiation
3. Due Diligence
4. Integration

Strategy

The strategy-development phase is the genesis of the acquisition process. Why does the distributor leadership want commit large amounts of capital and considerable management effort to the risky undertaking of buying other companies? How do acquisitions fit into the owners' plan for their investment? How do acquisitions fit into management's strategic plan for the business? How much money can the business afford to risk in making acquisitions? How much borrowing capacity does the company have, and how much debt is the company willing to take on? What is the company's backup plan if the acquisition program is not successful? What are the success criteria? In the target-selection process, what are the specific reasons for and against buying each company? How would any acquisition add value to the enterprise? If the acquisition were successful according to the company's criteria, what would be done next? After that? What if anything should be told to employees, lenders, and trading partners about the company's plans?

Negotiation

How will the courtship process be started? Who will plan and manage the process, and who will make the contacts? What will the targets be told about the company and its plans? What information is needed from the targets? Who will draft the nondisclosure agreement? Who will evaluate the information, structure the deal, and formulate an offer? Who will present the offer and negotiate with the target? Who will draft the terms sheet and the letter of intent? Who will negotiate with and secure commitments from potential lenders?

Due diligence

Who will plan, coordinate, and conduct the financial due diligence? Human resources? Logistics? Sales and marketing? Customer profitability analysis? Legal? Information systems?

Who will draft the definitive purchase agreement, employment agreements, and other documents? Who will evaluate the information and approve, renegotiate, or cancel the deal?

Integration

Who will plan and lead the integration effort? What will be done with the target company's employees? How will the customer relationships be protected? How will the vendor relationships be protected? How will the operations be combined? What will be done with the facilities? How will the information systems be integrated? How will financial reporting be done?

The mechanics of the process, such as the letter of intent and the definitive purchase agreement, fit into one or another of the four phases.

People often say it costs just as much to process a small transaction as a large one. This logic is sometimes used as a rationale to avoid buying small companies due to the overhead of processing even the smallest purchase. The high cost relates to the four steps, which must be managed thoroughly even if the transaction is fairly small and seems simple.

A distributor who has purchased many companies probably has a well-developed system for making acquisitions. A systematic approach would include having time-honored checklists, model documents, and spreadsheets ready to use. Thus, the experienced buyer may be able to speed the process along and keep costs down. Even the savviest buyers must complete the four steps with care, however.

The four phases of distributor acquisitions

Comparatively little has been written about buying and selling wholesale distribution businesses, in spite of the heavy M&A activity in distribution in recent years. A possible explanation is the notion that M&A is basically the same for all types of businesses. If you have experience buying manufacturing or service businesses, the thinking goes, you should have no trouble buying a distribution company (or a bank, or an insurance company). Another possible reason for the limited attention given in the literature to distributor transactions is the belief that buying distributors is a fairly simple, straightforward process.

I agree that the same four-step process applies to all types of transactions. But I disagree strongly with the idea that buying wholesaler-distributors is the same as buying manufacturers or other types of companies. Distributor acquisitions can be anything but simple and straightforward. An important wrinkle in the distributor M&A fabric is that the vast majority of distribution companies are owner-managed. The acquisition process is greatly complicated by the challenges of negotiating with an owner-manager, and performing due diligence on and integrating an owner-managed company.

The four-step process applies to all transactions, but no two deals are alike.

One of the reasons transactions take so long to complete, and that the amount of time needed is hard to predict, is that most or all of one step must be completed before the next step can be started. For example, the strategy phase must be completed prior to commencing the approach, courtship, and negotiations phase with a target. The meat and potatoes of due diligence can't be undertaken until the negotiations phase is complete. And the actual integration cannot start until due diligence is finished and the deal is closed. The planning for each step in the sequence can be completed and the resources can be lined up and ready to go, but nothing happens until the triggers are pulled.

The typical deal cannot follow a timeline with firm deadlines due to many obstacles, some of which are beyond the control of both buyer and seller. Transactions depend on the availability (and efficiency) of many outside parties such as attorneys, accountants, lenders, and government agencies. Delays at any one of them can cause scheduling problems with the others. As a result, this sequential process can and does break down, causing the next step to be delayed.

Don't rush the process

Unexpected delays often cause the planned closing date to be postponed. This may result in friction between buyer and seller, each of whom may be worried that the other is intentionally causing delays. Some transactions collapse simply due to the impatience of one or both parties.

The almost inevitable buildup of time pressure may tempt buyers to find ways to speed up the acquisition process. The due diligence phase may be the one most vulnerable to shortcuts. The buyer may decide, at his peril, to sprint toward the closing date by cutting out some of the scheduled due diligence work. An even more dangerous choice is the decision to ignore bad news coming from the due diligence work. The hasty buyer may conclude that getting the deal done on time is crucial and that small details cannot be allowed to stand in the way of progress.

The four phases are linked

The four steps in the acquisition process are chronological and are linked to one another. For example, the risk tolerances and resource evaluations from the strategy phase are the foundation of the negotiating phase. The resource limitations and the need to control risk place limits on how much can be paid for the target and how much can be borrowed to finance the deal.

The four steps are, on the other hand, mostly independent of one another. Once the strategy is developed and agreed upon, or once the negotiations are complete, they are seldom revisited. One step is completed before the next one is started.

Different people/advisors may handle each phase

Due to the independent nature of the four phases, different staff within the buyer's organization (and different outside resources) may handle each of the four phases of a transaction. Separating the steps is useful for several reasons.

For most buyers, the members of the acquisitions team must also carry on the duties of their regular job assignments while the acquisition is going on. Involvement in only one step of the transaction may make it easier for staff members to maintain focus on their regular work. Another advantage is the ability of the buyer's organization to work on more than one acquisition at a time. As deals move along through the four phases, the acquisition team is able to focus on one transaction at a time while the organization is keeping several irons in the fire.

Success and failure can be traced to process breakdowns

It always makes sense to avoid the buyer's trap of feeling that a certain deal has to get done, no matter what. The emotional attachment to a transaction, caused in part by the desire not to waste months of hard work, can be very powerful. Sometimes the management team wants to prove that its acquisition strategy was sound, even after learning that the target has unexpected problems. There may be an urge to prove that the buyer's organization can solve any problem the acquisition can throw at it.

One of the premises of this book is that the results from acquisitions of distributors often don't meet buyers' expectations. Examining the four-step acquisition process shows that breakdowns often occur. Success and failure seem to depend most on certain key elements in the acquisition process. If the buyer stumbles on those critical steps, he often falls down the staircase.

- **Strategy:** The acquisitive distributor makes acquisitions for the wrong reasons, or selects the wrong targets.

- **Negotiation:** The acquisitive distributor pays too much, borrows too much, or structures the transaction poorly.

- **Due diligence:** The acquisitive distributor doesn't dig deeply enough to avoid negative surprises, or ignores the bad news he does find.

- **Integration:** The acquisitive distributor does not carefully manage the acquired business and loses the critical employees and profitable customers he took so much trouble to acquire.

CHAPTER FOUR

Phase One: Strategy

"If you don't know where you're going, any road will take you there"

"Any Road" by George Harrison
• • • • • • • • • • • • • • • • •

Healthy living is a mission for most people, and losing extra weight is a good strategy to improve one's health. Other strategies to accomplish the healthy-living mission might include exercise and preventive health care. Let's say you set a strategic objective of losing 10 pounds. Some of the immediate benefits might be that your wardrobe fits and looks better and you have more stamina. The tactics for losing weight will vary from person to person: low carbs, passing on dessert, cutting out snacks, etc.

Profitable performance is a mission for most distribution companies, and growing sales is a good strategy for improving profits. Other strategies for accomplishing the profit mission might include cutting costs and improving asset management. Let's say you set a strategic objective of growing sales by 10% next year. Some of the immediate benefits might be that your company makes more money and your employees enjoy exciting new challenges. The tactics for making the acquisition will vary from company to company: making a small acquisition, hiring more sales reps, opening a new branch, etc.

My point is that growing sales is usually a good profit strategy, just as losing weight is a beneficial health strategy if you're overweight. And, while making acquisitions isn't the only way to grow, it is compatible with other growth strategies.

For many of us, dieting (along with other compatible health strategies) may be a necessity to achieve our health mission. For many wholesaler-distributors, making acquisitions (along with other growth strategies) is necessary to achieve the profit mission.

Still plenty of small distributors

Gurus with survey data and crystal balls have been warning small distributors about impending doom since the 1980s.

As mentioned previously, some popular advice boiled down to three options: get big, get specialized, or get out. Indeed, the critical mass needed to stay in the distribution game has increased in many industries. The specific reasons may vary, but the common threads often seen are that some of the largest customers have been making demands that only large suppliers can meet: integrated supply, global sourcing, national contracts, Internet auctions, electronic commerce, and vendor-managed inventory to name a few.

Ironically, technology advances seem to have given the little guys a reprieve: As the cost of technology dropped precipitously, small businesses were able to present the look and feel of a large company through their Internet presence, for example. Powerful computer systems have become affordable to smaller companies, and many small distributors have been able to harvest major productivity gains for their salespeople and other staff. On the other hand, some very large distributors have suffered setbacks (temporary or otherwise) from trying to implement overly ambitious technologies such as lights-out warehouses, customer relationship management software, and colossal enterprise systems.

One might argue that the days of very small distributors are numbered. But there are still lots of them, and many are doing quite well.

It's possible to stay small and be successful

One of the options available to small distributors who prefer to remain small is to specialize. There seem to be lots of places where specialization is possible and size doesn't matter too much. It's hard to imagine a very small steel distributor (but there are small distributors of tool steel, for example) or a very small distributor handling Wal-Mart. But there are good opportunities for those who don't want the risk or complexity of the kind of growth that leads to large-scale distribution.

Acquisitions are central to the strategy of most growing companies

Most distributors consider growth to be an imperative. Growth provides economies of scale, such as operational efficiencies and purchasing leverage with suppliers. Cash flow from profitable growth enables capital investments in facilities, equipment, and systems. Growth provides opportunities for employees to be challenged, to be recognized, and to advance.

Absent acquisitions, the three components of dollar growth are expansion of the economy (our customers buy more of our products and services), price increases (they pay more for what we sell), and market share penetration (we take away our competitors' customers). The annual sales forecasting and business planning process usually centers on trying to guess how much our customers will buy next year, what price increases the market will bear, and how much market share can we grab from the other guy.

During the period of industrial doldrums from 2000 to 2003, many wholesaler-distributors saw their customers buying less product, prices falling, and profitable market-share gains almost impossible to find. Competition was fierce due to an oversupply of many products and too many distributors and sales reps chasing too little business. Adding to the misery of this perfect storm were 9/11, the flood of product coming into North America from China, and the exodus of much domestic demand to plants overseas.

There is every reason to believe that the merger and acquisition market will remain active for distributors in the coming years. After a quiet period since 2000, activity has picked up considerably. Distributor CEOs indicate that they intend to buy as many companies in the next five years as they did in the preceding 10 years. (See Exhibit 4-1.)

EXHIBIT 4-1

Companies Acquired Last Ten Years and Expected Acquisitions Next Five Years

Number of companies acquired in last ten years:

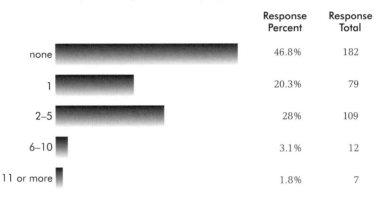

	Response Percent	Response Total
none	46.8%	182
1	20.3%	79
2–5	28%	109
6–10	3.1%	12
11 or more	1.8%	7

Total Respondents   389

Number of companies you expect to acquire in next five years:

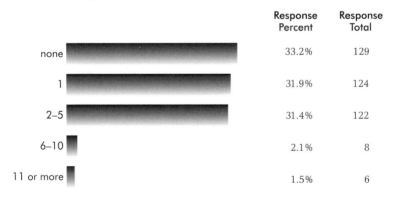

	Response Percent	Response Total
none	33.2%	129
1	31.9%	124
2–5	31.4%	122
6–10	2.1%	8
11 or more	1.5%	6

Total Respondents   389

Thus, an opportunity presents itself for the acquisitive distributor. In a sluggish growth environment, buying companies may prove to be the best—and maybe the only—growth path for distributors who want to maintain economies of scale in the years ahead. The perceived excess capacity of distribution in many lines of trade makes acquisitions viable and necessary for the ongoing profitability of the distribution channel.

Growth through acquisitions: not for everyone

"History has shown that mergers and acquisitions do little to help the long-term health and revenue growth of an organization," says Ram Charan, author of the 2004 book *Profitable Growth is Everyone's Business*. Charan points out that it isn't necessary to be the largest player to be successful, using the example of Colgate Palmolive's fight for retail shelf space against its much larger rivals Procter & Gamble and Unilever.

Acquisitions aren't for everyone. Buying companies is a risky proposition. Magazine articles about big company deals state that half or more of those blockbuster acquisitions are failures (they don't add to shareholder value). Distributor CEOs say that many of their acquisitions—one-third or more—did not meet their expectations.

It's fairly easy to measure success when analyzing public-company transactions, because the price of their shares reflects shareholder value. Analyzing the financial results of deals in which a privately held company is the acquirer is much more difficult; therefore, I asked 400-plus CEOs to talk about their most successful and least successful acquisitions. The information they shared illustrates the risks taken when buying someone else's company. Like an automobile engine, acquisitions have lots of places where leaks can occur.

There are growth options, other than acquisitions, for the faint of heart who desire to grow their distribution business. The traditional investments for jump-starting growth are always available: opening new branch locations, adding salespeople and new product lines. The problem with these strategies is that they add further capacity to what may already be an over-saturated market. The prospects for good returns on those investments are diminished without a corresponding reduction of competitive pressure.

The cost of growth

It's a fact of distributor life that the fuel of sales growth is cash flow from the profits of the business. Without adequate retained earnings to fund working capital, sales growth forces management to feed at the trough of bank loans. The typical distribution operating cycle (cash to finance inventory and receivables, less supplier financing) is about 90 days. Thus, it takes a permanent investment of 25 cents to finance one dollar of sales growth (warehouse sales). To grow sales by $4,000,000 you will have to reinvest $1,000,000 of after-tax profits, or borrow it from your banker if you can.

Good growth, bad growth: customer profitability

An underlying assumption of growth is that the additional sales will be profitable. Ram Charan makes the case that some forms of growth are bad for the business and must be avoided.

Customer profitability analysis (CPA) provides hard evidence of the operating profits generated by growth. Rather than looking only at additional sales revenue or gross profit dollars, CPA gives managers a reliable estimate of the operating profit of individual transactions, customers, or groups of customers. By identifying and isolating the additional transactions (or prospective transactions), management can understand the profits (or losses) resulting from added sales.

My book *More to the Bottom Line* provides detailed information about CPA tools for distributors. Software packages and professional guidance are available if you don't have the internal resources to conduct a customer profitability audit.

Reasons distributors give for making acquisitions

Distributor CEOs usually cite one of the following reasons for making a particular acquisition:

- To enter a new geographic market.
- To add a new product line or service.

- To eliminate a troublesome competitor.

- To access desired customers.

- To obtain quality salespeople.

- To add volume to achieve critical mass in a market they are already in.

- To access a desired supplier's product line.

Linking acquisitions to distributor strategy

The driving force of a distribution business is what brings the company together and gives it unified direction in the marketplace. The business could not build a strategy without a single, powerful driving force. The driving force may be intangible and invisible but, for successful distributors, it's a reality and it keeps the organization from going off in too many multiple directions.

Evergreen Consulting has assisted numerous distributor management teams with their strategic planning process. Our conclusion is that the driving force of nearly all distribution businesses is one of two possibilities:

1. A special understanding of a particular group of products (and services).

2. A deep understanding of the needs of a particular group of customers.

A well-conceived business concept is what makes one distributor distinctively different from its competitors. For example, a particular electronic distributor's business concept may be to stock hard-to-find items for specialized applications and charge a premium for them. A competitor's concept may be to carry popular, fast-moving items and offer them at low prices. A third competitor may focus on a sophisticated catalog and Internet-based ordering system, while a fourth may concentrate on value-added services such as kitting and technical support.

One-page strategic plan for distributors

The mental image of a strategic plan for some of us is a huge, overstuffed three-ring binder and flow diagrams as confusing as an M.C. Escher drawing. A distributor's strategic plan need not be as thick as the Manhattan telephone directory.

I advocate a strategy simple enough to describe on one piece of paper. That is not to say that the plan isn't carefully thought out, researched, tested, and documented. It is critical that every player on the team understands what the coach is trying to do. The leadership has to explain the plan clearly enough that each responsible individual knows what his role is and what he has to do to make the plan work.

A one-page strategic summary outlines the products/services, customer segments, and geographic markets the leaders have decided to focus on and, importantly, those that will receive little or no emphasis. Much of good planning is deciding what not to pursue.

Clarity of the distributor's strategy and adherence to a distinctive business concept help the acquisitive distributor determine what kinds of businesses are ideal targets to acquire and where they are located. The right targets will match up with the acquirer's strategy and business concept, fit into the geographic pattern, and address the buyer's strengths and weaknesses.

Distributor acquisition strategy: success factors

The Hedgehog Concept

Jim Collins, author of the immensely popular book *Good to Great*, talks about the difference between the fox, who focuses on and loses focus on many things, and the hedgehog, who concentrates on one big thing. He contends that foxes may have good companies, but hedgehogs build great companies by using their clarifying advantage.

Lily pads

Consider the greater likelihood of a successful acquisition when jumping from your business "lily pad" only to one of the adjacent lily pads in your pond instead of trying to jump to a whole new pond.

It seems obvious to me that a local distributor in Michigan would be courting disaster by acquiring a distributor in Florida. It appears equally dangerous that a small distributor of foodservice products would buy an industrial parts distributor. The nearest lily pad for the Michigan company might be an acquisition of a distributor of the same product lines in another city in Michigan, or perhaps nearby in Ohio. The foodservice distributor's nearest lily pad could be a distributor of the types of paper products or janitorial supplies used by his current customers.

I believe that it's a safer to acquire a nearby company that will get enough of your attention rather than choose a distant target that will be harder to visit. A good rule of thumb is that the company be close enough to drive to and back from in one day. Many of us will go to great lengths to avoid a trip involving an exhausting drive, an expensive flight, or an overnight stay.

Stick to the knitting

Tom Peters and Bob Waterman became famous years ago with their best-selling *In Search of Excellence*. The book was about companies they studied and what made those companies so much better than most, at least at the time the book was written. One of their concepts was called "stick to the knitting."

Distributors can help to minimize risk by acquiring businesses whose products, services, and customer segments are familiar to them. An acquisition target that has an incompatible business concept or strategy can be difficult to manage or may diffuse the focus of the existing business.

Some acquisitions are intended to bring in new products, new services, new customer segments, new geographic markets, etc. That makes perfect sense if the company is otherwise compatible, and it seems most sensible to introduce only one new element at a time (as opposed to a totally new product/service, a totally new geography, or a totally new customer segment all at once).

Risk tolerance

Management must face up to the amount of risk it is willing to take when working out its acquisition strategy.

A large acquisition is obviously riskier than a small one. A turnaround situation has a greater risk of failure than a profitable target, although the purchase price of the former may be enough that even a complete failure would not cause significant problems for the acquirer. I suggest evaluating the risk in two dimensions.

First, how much capital is the buyer risking as a percentage of its net worth? A buyer with a strong balance sheet (little debt in relation to total assets, a high degree of liquidity, and a generous reserve of borrowing availability) can afford a great deal more risk than a weak buyer. The capital at risk includes the purchase price, obligations assumed, debt guarantees, contingent liabilities, working capital to be invested, and needed capital expenditures.

Second, what is the likelihood that the acquisition will meet the buyer's expectations? Using scenario planning, estimates can be made of how the acquisition will perform based on various events such as loss of key contracts or major customers, loss of key employees, loss of critical suppliers, etc. Contingency plans should include the cost of replacing important staff, providing interim executives, and other identifiable risks. Consideration should be given to the cost of settling possible disputes with the sellers in the event of claims against them.

Many blockbuster acquisitions backfire. CEOs are sometimes tempted to try to double the size of their business in one transaction. Some of the most successful acquirers engage in a continuous stream of bite-sized transactions, each representing only a sliver of the acquirer's net worth.

A patient acquisitive distributor, chugging along with 3% annual growth, could consider making one small acquisition a year, each adding only 5% to the company's sales revenues. With a total growth rate of 8% (3% organic plus 5% from acquisitions), the company would double in size in only nine years. Without the acquisitions, at a 3% growth rate it, would take 24 years to double the size of the business.

Scarcity of good salespeople, branch and sales managers

There are usually one or two distributors in a given market that stand out in terms of their employees, the customers they serve, and the product lines they handle. These elite distributors may not have a dominant market share, or even be the largest in their market. But they have the lion's share of desirable customers and suppliers. They have an excellent reputation. In almost every case these elite distributors have the best salespeople in the market. In many lines of trade, except for those that are virtually totally consolidated, the elite distributors will be owner-managed.

How did these distributors capture the customers everyone else wants? In most instances the answer centers on the quality of the salesforce. There may a notable exception here and there—such as the distributor with an exclusive, prized product line. I would think that this type of exception would be rare.

Outstanding distributor salespeople are a rare breed, combining a strong work ethic, brainpower, and a high level of people skills. A recent book, *Primal Leadership*, by Richard Boyatzis (of Case Weatherhead School of Management, where I used to teach), Daniel Goleman, and Annie McKee, describes the characteristics of individuals who have a high degree of EI, or emotional intelligence. Salespeople who function at this level are able to maintain strong working relationships with customers over a long time period to track down and close deals with profitable new customers ("hunters"). These celebrated sales professionals are well paid, often on a straight-commission basis. People with this skill set could succeed at selling intangibles (investments, insurance). Therefore, attracting and retaining their services requires a generous compensation package. Only the best companies can attract and hold on to people of this caliber. Why are they so important? They are the key to finding and keeping large, profitable customers.

I also want to make a point about the scarcity of truly effective branch and sales managers in distribution. Collins notes that "Greatness does not depend on size" and "Highly diversified firms and conglomerates will rarely produce great results." He notes General Electric as an exception because that company develops first-rate general managers extremely well—a source of great pride for GE. Unfortunately, development of top-quality branch managers and sales managers is *not* a source of pride for many distributors. Most acquisitive distributors don't have a reserve of seasoned managers to plug into newly acquired companies. It is important to identify the winners in acquired companies and to hang on to them.

Small number of truly profitable customers

Customer profitability analysis demonstrates that, for most distributors, a small number of customers generate a large proportion of total operating profits. In many cases, detailed analysis shows that as few as 20% of customers provide nearly all of the operating profits. They must be protected at all costs. The few top salespeople usually are those who handle the small number of high-profit accounts.

The real value in most distributor acquisitions is securing long-term business relationships with high-profit customers. I will propose a simple valuation method based on the ongoing operating profit stream from these accounts. Conversely, a handful of large customers actually can cost a distributor money. There may be legitimate business reasons for subsidizing these customers, and in some instances they can be turned around. The largest groups of customers, which tend to be medium- and low-volume accounts, generate a small profit or a small loss.

Establishing acquisition criteria

When looking for new employees, too many executives fall in love with the idea of hiring a prospect during the interview. Perhaps we see ourselves in that person, or we think we would enjoy working with and getting to know him or her better. Instead of writing the job description first and searching for someone who has what we need, we find someone we like and then write the job description around what that individual has to offer. Do we get someone we like? Yes. Do we hire a person who can do what needs to be done? Not necessarily.

Many acquisition opportunities present themselves in the same random way that a job candidate appears for an interview.

We hear about an acquisition opportunity from a supplier, an employee, or a friend. The phone rings and a voice on the line, sometimes a business broker, may tell us a story about a company for sale. If we go ahead with a meeting, we might just fall in love with the idea of buying that company. We find a company we're attracted to and create our strategy around the target.

I advocate a proactive, not reactive, approach. With our one-page strategy and our business concept firmly in mind, we write criteria for an acquisition, or acquisitions, that will line up nicely with what we already have and where we want to go. We want to maximize the likelihood of success and minimize the possibility of failure, and we need to assure ourselves that, in the unlikely event of failure, we will not have done lasting damage to our existing business.

An amazing acquisition opportunity occasionally comes over the transom. I'm not saying that those should be ignored. Buying a competitor in an important market may have great profit potential—or it may be imperative to acquire a company to keep a rival out of a key market. (The same logic holds if a gifted salesperson walks in the door. Our philosophy was always to grab a great salesperson when the opportunity appeared. We always found plenty for him or her to do and never regretted it.)

True story

An industrial supplies distributor approached selected distributors in nearby markets to add specific product lines. The owner-managers were very congenial but, in most cases, had no real idea of what they wanted to do with their companies.

The owners who were willing to consider selling had unrealistic ideas about the value of their businesses. Their general expectation was to get enough money to take good care of all of the various family owners.

The buyer had to expand the focus from product lines to categories in order to significantly open up the number of prospective targets.

Advice to buyers: Buying from an owner-manager can be frustrating and often fruitless. Some companies just aren't for sale, even though the owners may lead you to believe otherwise; such deals won't get done even if you offer them everything they are asking for. Don't have too narrow of a focus, for example, looking only for distributors of specific product lines. It's better to have a broader scope in order to have enough viable targets.

Identifying targets that meet the acquisition criteria

Creating a list of target companies that meet your acquisition criteria is easy if you do your homework. The homework assignment is simple: Decide on the criteria first; make a list of the candidates second. The criteria will include the following:

- Industry (major product lines, key suppliers, services offered).

- Customer segments (industry specialization, large or small accounts).

- Sales method (outside sales, direct marketing, Internet sales).

- Size (estimated sales volume, number of employees).
- Geography (area covered, overlaps with existing business).
- Financial condition (growing and profitable, stable, struggling).
- Reputation (well regarded or otherwise).
- Management (good people in place or changes needed).

A good set of criteria enables you to narrow the field before starting out. That way you can focus your information gathering on companies most likely to meet your criteria and have a strategic fit with your business.

Obtaining information from the Internet and other sources

Information gathering is really a weeding-out process. The general idea is to come up with a short list of acquisition targets worth contacting to start a courtship process.

There is so much information available today that you don't need to wear out your shoes or even buy a tank of gas to do some serious research about target companies. I am referring, of course, to the Internet. Many business executives, and nearly everyone under the age of 30, are at least acquainted with the power of search engines such as Google, Yahoo, and some others.

When speaking before groups of business executives, if time allows, I enjoy presenting a 30-minute crash course on becoming an Internet search expert. I got my training personally from Sam Richter, President of the James J. Hill Reference Library in St. Paul. If you don't know about this library, I urge you to log on to their website, www.jjhill.org. My training focuses on the "hidden Internet," the sites and material that search engines cannot take you to. Some of the best research information is available only to subscribers, although these can be tapped at little or no cost if you subscribe or go through a library that has a subscription.

It is possible to review archives of all old web pages, even for businesses who think they removed those documents from the Internet. Local business or community newspapers can be electronically scanned for articles about a business or its managers, and court filings and many other legal documents including financial information can be obtained. Evergreen Consulting has trained CPAs on use of the Internet for client research, including preparation to serve as an expert witness. We have trained trade association executives on Internet use to research prospective members and salespeople on using the Internet prepare for meetings with customers and prospects.

Aside from the Internet, industry people have access to the most valuable information of all. Your own employees and trading partners, including supplier representatives and others, have a wealth of information about companies you may be interested in acquiring now or in the future. I encourage you to keep a file about each company you have any interest in. Ask about the companies as you go about your daily business and file your notes away for future use. You'll be well prepared when and if you decide to contact the owners.

The culmination of the research phase of your work is a short list of acquisition prospects that are probably in line with your strategy and are affordable, and therefore have a decent chance of adding to your top line and profits. Now there are two big questions: Is your information accurate? Do they have any interest in selling?

Cultivating targets

As you already surmised, I don't believe you need to pay an outside expert to do homework you can best do for yourself. With your knowledge of the industry and wealth of contacts, you can obtain better information, and faster, than any outsider could. Of course, you may want to hire an outside firm to do the research because you simply don't have the time or discipline to do it, or that you feel more comfortable with professional guidance. In such cases it is certainly better to pay someone else rather than forfeit the opportunity for profitable growth through acquisitions.

Cultivating targets is an art, not a science. In some cases the distributor CEO is in an excellent position to do this. Distributor

CEOs tend to know one another through trade association activities or supplier councils. It certainly helps if a positive relationship already exists and can be expanded upon. This type of contact is strictly owner-to-owner.

Some obstacles can block this pathway. One is fear or suspicion of the acquirer. The target company may worry about the motives of a competitor who may be fishing for information about customers, suppliers, or employees. A second possibility is the prospective target's need to put a happy face on a bad situation. People don't like to reveal to the competition that they are struggling.

A third and very common situation is owners who have different ideas about selling. Unfortunately, you won't find too many situations where there is a sole proprietor, or one owner who can speak for the rest of the owners. Many wholesale distribution companies are intergenerational (father and son) or even multigenerational (grandparents, kids, and grandchildren). The reason some of these family companies were never sold is a lack of agreement (or lack of communication) among the aunts, uncles, cousins, and others who own pieces of the family pie.

In some of these situations, which may include a mixture of suspicion, fear, and a dysfunctional family of owners, the acquisitive distributor needs a helping hand to cultivate the prospect. I have a story about this type of situation.

I have a colleague in Florida whom I've known for 20 years, since the days when he was a managing partner of the local office of a national accounting firm. He just happens to be one of those rare people who are very savvy with numbers, great with people, and persistent as hell. He went into the M&A business when he got tired of being an accountant. One of the companies where I sit as a director uses my friend to cultivate acquisition prospects. He has been doing this for at least seven years and has facilitated at least four excellent deals so far. Each one of those deals has worked out successfully. The CEO knew every one of the sellers. What role did my friend the M&A guy play?

Most important, he developed a personal relationship with each of the sellers. He sat with them and listened to their stories. They recognized his competency, trustworthiness, and experience, so they asked for his advice. Eventually, they opened up to him and told him about their problems, their needs, and their hopes for the business. He was able to bring them to the table and structure some creative deals that enabled them to sell the controlling interest in their businesses, retain a minority interest for a period of time, continue working at the company, enable their partner to take his money and retire, get all their debts paid off, secure jobs for their kids, take care of their loyal employees, etc. Did my friend earn his keep? Yes! These deals would probably never have happened without his help. You need to know that he worked with one of these sellers for three years before the deal was put together.

I should also tell you about the owners he talked with who never sold. There's the guy in New York who was basically waiting for his father to die before he could sell the company (his father eventually did pass away, but the son decided to keep the business after all). There's the company in Ohio with two brothers who don't speak to each other except through their uncle and are gradually running the business into the ground. There are the two 50-50 partners who can't agree on sale of the company because they charge all of their personal expenses to the business.

The courtship process can be frustrating, time-consuming, and ultimately fruitless. The CEO has a business to run and may be impatient by nature, as so many CEOs tend to be. Cultivation is a job that is often best handled by an outsider whom the target can feel comfortable with. In some cases it may be sensible to pay the outsider an hourly fee and a reasonable success fee when a deal is consummated. It isn't always necessary to pay a huge "investment banking" fee (a percentage of the purchase price) to an advisor for this type of work.

True story

An advisor to Wayne Huizenga expressed her concern at the price he was about to pay for a chain of video stores being acquired by his firm, Blockbuster Video. He was building a national chain of retail locations and needed the acquisition in question to execute his strategy on schedule.

As a masterful acquirer and business builder (Blockbuster and Waste Management), Huizenga was able to sense when paying a large premium was the best move for his company.

Not everyone has the foresight and skills of a Huizenga. Some national distribution chains have gotten themselves in big trouble by overpaying for the wrong company, in the wrong place, at the wrong time.

Huizenga knew his limitations as well as his strengths. When his companies did not have needed expertise in house, he brought in professional advisors or hired experts from successful companies to build capabilities.

Advice to buyers: Paying a premium price for the right company may be the best move. If an acquisition has great strategic importance, such as preventing a competitor from entering a market, it may pay to offer the price necessary to make the deal. Even the greatest deal makers may not be masters of skills such as due diligence and integration. Bring in the best people you can to do this work.

Use of outside advisors to find targets

Speaking of huge fees, investment banking types sometimes do play a crucial role in putting an acquisition together.

You can expect to pay a hefty fee if you ask an outside advisor to go out and find targets for you, cultivate the prospects, assist you in negotiating and closing the deal, and perhaps to line up the financing. This type of work is speculative, time consuming, and relies on leveraging contacts and experience gained during a lifetime of work. It's customary to pay a percentage of the purchase price to a real-estate broker to match up buyers and sellers (of course the seller usually pays the fee), and it is customary to pay a percentage of the purchase price to a business broker. If you are the buyer, and you are the one who engages the advisor, the fee will be your responsibility.

What fee arrangement is customary? I have seen people starting out in the field who are anxious to take on assignments for low fees, but the usual request by an experienced firm (as opposed to someone working on his own) is a monthly retainer to commence the search. A typical amount would be $3,000 to $5,000 per month, for a minimum of four to six months. The advisor needs that much time to establish criteria, conduct research, and to contact and qualify targets. The up-front fees will usually be credited against the success fee if a deal is completed.

A long-standing formula for success fees as a percentage of the purchase price is the Lehman formula (as in Lehman Brothers, the investment banking firm). The formula is 5% of the first million dollars, 4% of the second million, 3% of the third million, 2% of the fourth million, and 1% of everything over four million. There has been much inflation since this formula was first used, so some investment bankers ask for multiples of the Lehman formula and have formulas of their own. Like almost everything else in business, these fees are negotiable. One would expect to find more flexibility at a smaller firm. Most deals for acquisitive distributors are small transactions that would not interest a large firm (and even if they did, the firm might assign its least experienced people). A handful of firms specialize in distribution.

Boards of large public companies sometimes hire an investment banker to provide a "fairness opinion" to validate the management's pricing on a transaction. A small acquisitive distributor usually doesn't need this type of outside assurance, but it is helpful to get input from an experienced person to help avoid a costly mistake, or hastily passing up a deal with good potential.

The CEO's vision for the business

If the acquisitive distributor is an owner-managed business, the pressure on the CEO to make acquisitions is mostly internal rather than external. The CEO of a public company faces demands from the board and investors for steady growth and profit increases. A guide word for CEOs in that environment is "accretion": How would a proposed acquisition affect projected earnings per share? What would be the likely effect on the share price?

Fortunately, most CEOs don't face those pressures. However, one thing most do have in common is a powerful ego and a desire to win. The pathway to sales growth, profitable growth, often leads the CEO to become an acquisitive distributor.

The CEO's vision for the distribution business and the company's strategy have started the process of identifying targets and cultivating prospects. Some interesting acquisition opportunities have been uncovered and the owners are willing to talk about a deal.

The negotiation process has begun.

CHAPTER FIVE

Phase Two: Negotiation

"In business, you don't get what you deserve; you get what you negotiate"

Chester Karass
. . . .

Have you ever read a book or taken a course on negotiating skills? Many of us have, judging from the popularity of Donald Trump's *The Art of the Deal* and also the frequency of direct-mail brochures advertising one-day training courses held in crowded airport hotel meeting rooms. I still see Chester Karass advertisements in airline magazines. He must be onto something, after running essentially the same ad for more than 20 years.

I've never been a fan of negotiation ploys, gimmicks, and trickery. But it's good to know about these things so you can spot the method being used when someone else is playing games with you.

I believe that putting together a good business deal depends on following a well designed process, having as much useful information as possible, and understanding both your needs and those of the people on the other side. Besides knowing the basics and having common sense, most of the rest is the stuff you learned (or should have learned) in kindergarten.

Process

According to *Lessons from Master Acquirers: A CEO Roundtable on Making Mergers Succeed* (Harvard Business School Press, 2000), the deal cycle must be carefully managed:

1. Screen potential deals; not just the deal at hand.
2. Reach initial agreement before determining price.
3. Link due diligence to business planning.
4. Set final terms, while being sure to have alternatives to this deal.
5. Achieve closure: Close quickly.

Lessons from Master Acquirers suggests explaining the "plot" (of the deal) to the participants and requiring the teams to conduct daily roundtable discussions so everyone can hear progress, issues, and concerns of the group.

The beauty of a well designed process is that it keeps you on track, prevents mistakes, forces you to do things in the proper order, and is flexible enough to adjust to different situations. We all know that no battle plan remains intact after engagement with the other side, but it sure helps to have a structure to fall back on and to have everyone working together on the same page.

I have offered a process with four major phases and a series of steps in each phase. This approach isn't best for all transactions, but it can be adapted to work for most situations the acquisitive distributor will encounter. Your attorney and accountant may have their own ideas and may not agree with one another. I don't necessarily want to contradict the advice of your other advisors, but keep in mind that their experiences may be with other clients (doctors buying medical practices, individuals buying franchises, etc.) that have nothing to do with buying a distribution business.

True story

The top executive of a large electrical distributor has made several acquisitions to grow geographically. He's worked hard to maintain the integrity of the companies he bought while recognizing the need to economize. He needs to grow to survive and needs to make acquisitions to grow.

This acquirer has paid more than he should have but does not regret it. He has sometimes tried too hard to sell himself on a deal in due diligence and has learned to walk away, especially after things didn't turn out to be as described by the seller.

He knows that people at all levels of the acquired company must be comfortable with the buyer. The less their lives are interrupted during integration, the more comfortable they will be. He tries to keep the same product lines so the sales people don't need to relearn. He is flexible with human resources issues such as vacation policy.

The acquirer is upfront about the need to let some people go, and will pay a monetary incentive to needed people who stay during the integration period, even though they will be leaving later on.

This buyer tries to buy companies using the same information system as the one used by his main business.

Advice to buyers: Don't bend over backwards to make a deal. Stick to your plan. Don't pay up front.

Initiating the discussion

Assuming now that you or a third party representing you has approached the targets on your short list, the process has started. The next step is developing a relationship with the prospect that will lead to the critical question: "Do you, Mr. Seller, have enough interest in selling your business to me to sign a non-disclosure agreement, and to provide some information that will enable me to present an offer?"

Leading up to this important conversation, you as buyer need to present a compelling case for why the proposed acquisition makes sense for the seller. The buyer explains his vision for his business and his expansion ideas and why he feels the seller's company fits in with his plans. The seller needs to understand what the buyer intends to do with his company, whether or not the buyer wants him and his employees to stay with the business, whether it will be relocated, how the business will be operated, whether the name will be changed, what new suppliers and products will be available to the customers, what suppliers will be eliminated, how the people will be compensated, whether the people will have advancement opportunities in the acquiring company, and so forth.

The buyer is wise to be as open as possible with the seller and to be totally honest. There is a conflict between the desire to win the seller's support for going ahead to the next step and the risk of turning the seller off if he disagrees with the buyer's plans.

Cultivating the seller: starting to structure the deal

At some point the seller will need to explain the ownership structure of his company. Assume you are dealing with an owner-manager who does not own or control all of the stock. This person may not have the authority to sell his own stock, let alone sell the assets of the business. Many closely held corporation shareowner agreements restrict the sale of shares to outside parties.

Deal-savvy distributor CEOs indicate that they rarely purchase the stock of companies they acquire (see Exhibit 5-1).

Nearly all buyers prefer to purchase the assets of the seller's company for two powerful reasons.

1. Purchasing stock can result in the buyer's assuming the corporation's contingent liabilities, including income tax, sales tax or other taxes; penalties and interest uncovered in tax audits; product liability claims, employment practices liability and other legal claims; unrecorded debts

EXHIBIT 5-1
Use of Cash or Your Company's Stock

	Always	Usually	Sometimes	Rarely	Never	Response Average
1. Cash payment	69% (83)	26% (31)	3% (4)	1% (1)	2% (2)	1.41
2. Company stock	0% (0)	4% (3)	5% (4)	11% (9)	80% (66)	4.68
3. Combination of cash and stock	0% (0)	6% (5)	8% (6)	13% (10)	73% (56)	4.52
					Total Respondents	122

of all kinds; labor contract obligations; retirement plan and other fringe-benefit plan liabilities; environmental claims, and many more. Warranties and representations from the seller can be made to provide some protection to the buyer, but most buyers are not willing to take these risks when buying stock.

2. Purchasing assets can give the buyer favorable income tax treatment. The buyer has more latitude in allocating the purchase price to assets that can be quickly written off against otherwise taxable income.

Distributor CEOs with deal experience also state that they do not like to purchase less than 100% ownership of companies they acquire (see Exhibit 5-2).

Of course, purchase of less than 100% means that the buyer must buy stock, not assets. Second, ownership of less than 100% means there are obligations to other shareholders. The owner of even a tiny minority interest in a corporation may have significant shareholder rights. Even though this owner may not be able to influence the company's affairs by electing a member of the board of directors, many courts will bend over backwards to protect minority shareowners from perceived abuses of power by the other owners.

EXHIBIT 5-2

Ownership Strategy – Percentage Interest Obtained

	Always	Usually	Sometimes	Rarely	Never	Response Total
1. 100% ownership acquired	76% (90)	19% (23)	4% (5)	0% (0)	0% (0)	118
2. 80–99% ownership acquired	2% (1)	7% (4)	17% (10)	7% (4)	68% (40)	59
3. 51–79% ownership acquired	3% (2)	0% (0)	14% (8)	7% (4)	76% (45)	59
4. less than 51% ownership acquired	3% (2)	0% (0)	3% (2)	5% (3)	88% (52)	59
					Total Respondents	122

I would like to share a story of how buying less than 100% of a target company's stock can work in the buyer's best interests. The target company, a distributor in an adjacent state, had two shareholders who worked in the business: a 40% owner and a 60% owner. The 60% owner wanted to sell his interest and retire; the 40% owner wanted to hold onto his stock and continue working, but didn't have the money needed to buy out his 60% partner and felt he was too close to retirement to take on a great deal of debt. He also did not want to run the business without enough capital to make investments and expand. Our client, the acquirer, was willing to buy the 60% interest and become a business partner with the minority owner for five years. The minority owner served as president of the business. The acquirer invested in the company and assisted the president in building the business. The minority owner's stock was purchased five years later according to a formula which gave the seller some appreciation based on the increase in the net worth of the company. The arrangement led to a smooth leadership transition and excellent growth and profit results during the five-year period. The arrangement worked so well that the same client made a similar deal when he expanded into yet another state.

The technique of purchasing a partial interest in these two deals is really just a two-step or deferred purchase of the entire company. In each transaction the buyer had a firm arrangement to purchase the balance of the stock not later than a certain date, and to pay a price based on a formula related to the company's interim results.

The question of deal structure needs to be handled early in the acquisition process. The buyer and seller need to understand the other party's needs concerning buying stock versus assets and the possible advantages of purchasing a partial interest in the company.

Non-disclosure agreements. The first document both parties will sign is a non-disclosure agreement designed to protect the confidentiality of the information the seller will provide. The buyer typically agrees to keep the information private, not to make copies, to return the information on request, and not to use the information to harm the seller. Non-disclosure agreements usually carefully describe the information and provide for the possibility that the seller may already have some of the information because it has been made public by the seller. The buyer usually tries to protect himself by stating that he would have to comply with a court order to divulge the information. The buyer generally prepares the non-disclosure agreement and the seller asks his legal advisor to review it. The buyer is trying to be as helpful as possible at this stage of the process, and the non-disclosure agreement is usually written so that the seller's lawyer will find it acceptable as presented.

Information gathering. The acquisitive distributor may present a summary of requested information following the signing of the non-disclosure agreement. It is helpful if the buyer puts the request in writing to avoid the need to come back later for more information.

I suggest using a short (non-intimidating) form and avoid asking for too many details. This is not due diligence. The sole purpose of asking for this information is to prepare an offer. The offer will be based on the summary information provided by the seller. If an agreement is reached, the buyer will have an opportunity to verify all of the information.

Terms sheet. After digesting the information provided by the seller and analyzing the synergies of combining the companies (as well as assessing the risks), the acquisitive distributor is faced with a decision to go ahead and make an offer or pull the plug. If the buyer did his homework, it isn't too likely that the information provided by the seller will cause the buyer to walk away at this point.

If there are unpleasant surprises, ask for clarification and an explanation. If you're not satisfied with the answers, I urge you to move on to other, more attractive opportunities. If you decide not to make an offer, meet with the seller personally and provide as much of an explanation as you can. The situation may change and the target may become attractive in the future. Try to keep the door open for future conversations and do whatever you can to monitor changes in the seller's business. Be sure to return any information the seller provided and to enforce the confidentiality agreement with any of your own people who worked on the deal with you. Make certain that no copies were made.

The terms sheet is a good way to start the ball rolling with the seller. What you put on the terms sheet makes the deal come to life for the seller. He will start to visualize the transaction and to estimate how much money will be in his pocket after paying off his liabilities, taxes, and transaction expenses. The seller may ask his accountant to help with the analysis. He may want to compare his annual cash flow before and after the deal. The terms sheet is non-binding; your lawyer may want you to be sure that it clearly says so.

The terms sheet includes a small number of key pieces of information, such as how much the buyer is willing to pay, what the buyer intends to purchase, any liabilities the buyer is willing to assume, and when and how the buyer intends to pay (such as seller financing or an earn-out, basing a portion of the ultimate purchase price on subsequent performance. Other possible items are the basic terms of any real-estate leases or employment agreements that the buyer has in mind.

Projections. The basis of determining purchase price is the company's projected cash flow under the buyer's ownership. The bedrock for the cash-flow computation is the earnings projection, with add-backs and adjustments. Add-backs and adjustments are explained later in this chapter.

Sales growth assumptions. The starting point is projected sales, based on information provided by the seller, analysis of historical data, and other information such as expectations of price increases, gains in market share, and growth in the economy. The buyer needs to be cautious about possible losses in sales due to the change in ownership, such as strong customer relationships with the owner-manager or the potential loss of key sales reps.

Margin assumptions. Margin assumptions need to be tempered by the possibility of intense price competition caused by the loss of key sales reps to competitors.

Please see the chapter about customer profitability analysis for further information. My advice is to carefully review each of the high-profit accounts individually when preparing a forecast of sales and margins.

Operating expense assumptions. Buyers sometimes assume they can quickly bring the operating expenses of an acquired company in line with their existing business. This may be more difficult and take longer than expected. An exception is the opportunity to acquire a competitor in a market where the buyer already operates and meld the operations immediately. Other than exceptional cases, the conservative approach is to use historical expense ratios with add-backs and adjustments as outlined below.

Asset management assumptions. Cash flow is very sensitive to a distributor's ability to turn inventory, collect receivables, and negotiate favorable payment terms with suppliers. A buyer cannot assume that his management will translate into immediate improvement at the company being acquired. It is much safer to assume asset turnover will not change much during the first year or two.

Supplier retention assumptions. The buyer needs to verify that important suppliers will approve the transfer of product lines to the buyer. Or the buyer may need to ask his suppliers to approve the sale of their lines in his new operation. There is a risk if the supplier refuses to support the distributor or decides to appoint additional distributors.

Employee retention assumptions. Customer profitability analysis will underscore the concentration of high-profit customers with a small number of outside sales reps. Pay attention also to the concentration of top customers with the owner-manager or another key manager. Hanging on to high-profit customers may be dependent on retaining key customer relationship employees.

Weight placed on recent performance. *Caveat emptor.* Beware of one excellent year preceded by several bad ones. A manager who pulls out all the stops for a sensational one-year performance may have penalized the company's ability to perform in the future (or maybe he was just lucky). The name of the game is sustainable, long-term performance. Look at the trend over at least three years, preferably five. Look especially at trends with the largest, most profitable accounts.

Add-backs and adjustments. The buyer tries to identify expenses the business incurs under the old ownership that the new owner will not incur. The premise is that the owner-manager charges some costs to his company that are greater than the new owner will have to pay (such as when the owner-manager draws a very high salary or charges above-market rent). The owner-manager may charge some costs to his company that are personal in nature and will not be continued under the new ownership. Examples might be country club dues, a lease for an expensive car, non-business travel. The amounts in the preceding examples are added back to the company's projected earnings.

The add-backs are deductions if the owner-manager pays some business costs out of his own pocket or if the company pays below-market prices for services provided by the owner-manager.

Experience has taught me to be very cautious about add-backs, especially ones that increase projected earnings, unless they are well documented and solid.

The buyer also looks for opportunities to enhance the company's earnings under his ownership. He may be able to improve gross trading margin through access to lower product costs from his suppliers or his buying/marketing group. The new owner may be confident that he can improve inventory turns, speed up collections, or avoid bad debts under his management. Other low-hanging fruit may appear to be reductions in fringe benefits costs, improvements in personnel productivity, etc. The improvements the buyer anticipates under his ownership are adjustments to be added to the company's projected earnings.

It's possible that some of the adjustments will be subtractions from projected earnings. The new owner may feel that the business was not properly insured under the old ownership and the increased premiums are negative adjustments. The new owner may want to improve the delivery fleet, install a new computer system, hire more salespeople, or relocate the business. These adjustments are also subtractions from projected earnings.

I appreciate the cautious optimism of buyers, but I'm skeptical about the tendency to overestimate the immediate improvements and minimize the cost of additional investments. The integration process takes patience and hard work, and it isn't always wise for the new owner to make immediate, dramatic changes. Some of the "low-hanging fruit" ideas may not be as easy to accomplish as the optimistic manager expects. He needs to study the situation closely before he acts, and there will be other important work to do during the integration process.

Acquiring a competitor in a market where the buyer already has a location is a special situation. Some people refer to such an acquisition as a "tuck-in," especially if the target company is much smaller than the buyer's. The new owner can combine locations, management, salespeople, and management information systems. These transactions can offer immediate cost savings. Documented, solid cost reductions (less any cost increases) are positive adjustments.

Price. Oscar Wilde said that a cynic is a man who knows the price of everything but the value of nothing. Not to be critical of the motives of others, I am skeptical about acquisition analysis focused entirely on deal prices.

In researching this book, I asked over 400 distribution executives for detailed information about their three largest acquisitions in the preceding 10 years. For the sake of encouraging participation and enabling comparisons, I kept my request simple: total price paid including debt assumed, sales at the time of acquisition, operating profit at the time of acquisition, and net book value of assets acquired.

The exhibit in the Appendix includes the ratios financial analysts thrive on: price paid as a percentage of sales (dependable but not very useful); price paid as a multiple of earnings (useful but not very dependable); price paid in relation to book value (not very useful and not very dependable).

The ratios are broken down by industry where there are enough responses to make a sensible computation. You can sort through these data, observe trends from year to year, and make comparisons among the various industries.

Private companies provided most (96%) of this information. It's hard to obtain these data from private firms, so most of the M&A comparisons you see in print are from public companies. This is the real world—what buyers actually paid and what they actually got for their money. I have two major problems with this type of analysis.

First, the quality of earnings information varies widely. Companies compute operating earnings in different ways. There is a lot of latitude in determining salaries, rent, interest, etc., between related parties such as owners and their companies. The same thing is true of the way net worth is computed. Sales are a good, objective number (except for the rare cases of some now-infamous public company scandals) but it's deceptive to compare purchase compared to sales for distribution companies. For example, in some lines of trade, low-margin direct shipments make up more than half of sales. It would appear that they sold their companies at low prices due to their inflated sales number compared to the same ratio for distributors who are almost all high-margin warehouse sales.

Second, terms are really important, especially in smaller deals. The seller's long-term consulting contract or compensation package, or the sweet rental deal on the warehouses he leases to the buyer, may constitute a large portion of the purchase price.

Since we are on the subject of pricing, I want to encourage you to read the chapter on customer profitability analysis. My argument is that analyzing the operating profit of the customers, especially the largest customers, is critical when valuing a distribution business. You are purchasing a stream of future operating profits, based on the assumption that you will continue doing business with the customers who provide most of the seller's operating profits. Aside from the price paid for assets such as inventory (which you could buy directly from the suppliers) and equipment (also easy to buy on the open market), the premium or goodwill the buyer pays is for the earning power of the business. In nearly all cases, the buyer will operate the company somewhat (or a lot) differently than the seller does. A later chapter talks about the different kinds of buyers, but I am focusing mostly on "strategic buyers" in this discussion because acquisitive distributors are strategic buyers.

True story

An industrial supplies distributor was encouraged by customers to acquire a particular competitor. The target was an underperforming branch of a larger distributor, owned in turn by a private equity firm.

The distributor used the services of an intermediary (a boutique investment banking firm) to approach the private equity firm and advise in the negotiations.

The distributor found that private equity firms are sharks ("We don't even swim in the same water") and that dealings can be nasty. With perseverance and good counsel, the deal will get done.

Advice to buyers: Hire a great advisor. A financial seller is different from a strategic seller.

Valuation methods

A respected way of calculating purchase price is the discounted cash-flow analysis, which scientifically applies net present value computations to expected future cash flows.

Thank goodness for spreadsheets, which make this work easy—maybe too easy, because the spreadsheets look really good and inspire confidence. Part of that confidence may be because they're prepared by really smart MBAs who are experts in doing this type of analysis. Here's a problem: Business guys who really want the deal to work provide the data that go into the spreadsheets. They come up with projected sales numbers, projected gross profit percentages, projected operating expense savings, and projected asset management improvements that are often unrealistic and sometimes off the wall.

To justify the purchase price, dealmakers have been known to tweak the numbers: bump sales up 1%, goose gross margin percentage by 1%, squeeze operating expenses by 1%, etc. The power of one percent! Distribution is a game of inches, where a 2% return on sales may be mediocre and a 4% return on sales may be stellar. That number tweaking is pretty scary if you think about the effect it has on projected operating earnings and cash flow. The small changes are magnified by the discounted cash-flow analysis. And if you still don't like the results, you can always play with the interest rates used to discount the cash flows.

True story

A medium-sized distributor of power transmission products has built his business in the slow-growth Toledo area by making acquisitions and selling on the Internet.

He has trouble dealing directly with owner-managers who cannot be objective about the value of their companies. They often look to the company to provide for them for the rest of their lives, as opposed to how much the business is worth.

He has spent hours of free consulting time helping owners improve companies he ultimately did not purchase due to inability to agree on price. Some sellers, he says, "don't even know how many customers they have."

The buyer has attended presentations by professional advisors helping owners to sell their companies. In one instance the advisor prepared slides and a brochure projecting that the $1 million business would achieve $14 million sales within eight years. The slick presentation was great, but the business plan was totally unrealistic.

This buyer, who signs every check at his company, likes to look through the seller's checkbook to see where the money is being spent.

His two best purchases were spinoffs from large manufacturing corporations who "weren't emotionally involved in what they were selling." He became a distributor for both companies, who tried distribution of their own products but changed their minds.

Advice to buyers: This acquirer has observed unrealistic valuations placed on distribution companies by sellers and their advisors. Don't be the first buyer to make an offer to a seller who has done his own valuation.

It has been said (*Harvard Business Review*, April 2004) that the "momentum of the transaction is hard to resist once senior management has the target in its sights." A mid-level manager at a *Fortune* 500 corporation, seasoned in acquisitions, told me, "Of course we have a well documented manual covering every stage of an acquisition including valuation" but, "Once senior management falls in love with a deal, we throw the playbook out the window; we will be told to get the deal done, no matter what."

A highly experienced M&A executive, referring to a particularly expensive acquisition, told me, "This is the last deal that we are going to let the CEO price." His team had done the analytical work and set deal parameters, but the CEO overrode their recommendations.

Distributors use a variety of valuation techniques. The following exhibit shows the amount of importance placed on several. (See Exhibit 5-3.)

EXHIBIT 5-3

Valuation Techniques

The amount of importance placed on the following valuation techniques.

	Important	Neither Important nor Unimportant	Unimportant	Don't Use	Response Average
1. Discounted cash flow	55% (70)	26% (33)	2% (3)	17% (21)	1.80
2. Seller's projections	21% (26)	40% (50)	25% (32)	14% (18)	2.33
3. EBITDA multiple/earnings multiple	68% (87)	20% (25)	6% (8)	6% (8)	1.51
4. Adjusted book value	46% (58)	29% (37)	17% (22)	8% (10)	1.87
5. Customer profitability analysis	63% (79)	21% (26)	9% (11)	8% (10)	1.62
6. Most recent year results	65% (82)	28% (35)	3% (4)	4% (5)	1.46
7. Most recent three years' results	81% (105)	15% (19)	1% (1)	3% (4)	1.26
8. Other	50% (10)	25% (5)	0% (0)	25% (5)	2.00
				Total Respondents	136

According to *Lessons from Master Acquirers*, financial acquirers are more successful than their corporate counterparts because they approach the acquisition process differently. I quote: "Fund investors treat deal management as a core part of their business conducted by a permanent group of experienced executives... [who] have a well established process they stick to." Many corporate managers treat acquisitions as a "march up the hill" exercise, whereas successful corporate acquirers "coordinate the different actors (senior managers, lawyers, investment bankers) throughout the process."

Harvard Business Review notes, "Many companies don't allow the negotiating manager to price the deal, for fear he will become emotionally invested and overpay...a higher-level manager will set a ceiling price."

My advice is to use discounted cash-flow analysis as only one of your valuation methods, to be sure you understand all of assumptions and truly think they are conservative, and to assure yourself that the discount rate used is also conservative. Finally, ask an expert to explain the concept to you until you're sure you understand terms like "discounted terminal value" and how they affect the results. Some bankers love this type of analysis, by the way, probably using it to verify that you will be able to repay the loan they are making to finance the transaction. That's great, but remember that you are the one who has to pay them back. It's your spreadsheet, it's your acquisition, and it's your money.

Earnings multiples are another popular way to value acquisitions. People love to talk about deals in relation to how many times earnings they paid (low) or got (high). The earnings multiples move up and down with fluctuations in the financial markets. Most deals are financed largely with borrowed money (see Exhibit 5-4).

Distributor CEOs finance 50% to 80% of the purchase price of most deals and borrow most of that money from banks (see Exhibit 5-5).

The more they can borrow, the further their cash investment will go. Theoretically, the more they can borrow, the more they are willing to pay for an acquisition. Many distributors use cash,

EXHIBIT 5-4

Financing Sources

	Always	Usually	Sometimes	Rarely	Never	Response Total
1. Bank debt	39% (46)	37% (44)	17% (20)	4% (5)	3% (4)	119
2. Mezzanine financing	1% (1)	2% (2)	17% (14)	12% (10)	67% (54)	81
3. Venture capital	0% (0)	0% (0)	5% (4)	11% (9)	84% (69)	82
4. Private equity	12% (10)	14% (12)	15% (13)	6% (5)	53% (46)	86
5. Seller financing	8% (8)	21% (20)	33% (32)	8% (8)	29% (28)	96
6. Earn outs/contingent payments	14% (13)	15% (14)	39% (36)	4% (4)	28% (26)	93
					Total Respondents	121

EXHIBIT 5-5

Amount Borrowed

Financing strategy – use of leverage.

	Always	Usually	Sometimes	Rarely	Never	Response Total
1. 0–20% equity; balance debt	19% (17)	38% (33)	6% (5)	8% (7)	30% (26)	88
2. 21–50% equity; balance debt	8% (7)	31% (26)	24% (20)	12% (10)	25% (21)	84
3. Combination of cash and stock	13% (10)	15% (11)	7% (5)	12% (9)	53% (40)	75
					Total Respondents	115

not their own stock, to pay for their acquisitions (see Exhibit 5-6).

Here's an example. Some bank loans are based on the borrower's cash flow, usually the cash flow for the trailing 12

EXHIBIT 5-6

Stock or Asset Purchase

Indicate how often your company uses the following methods to make and finance acquisitions. Purchase of assets or stocks:

	Always	Usually	Sometimes	Rarely	Never	Response Total
1. Purchase outstanding shares	2% (2)	10% (8)	24% (20)	16% (13)	48% (39)	82
2. Purchase assets	54% (63)	34% (40)	9% (10)	1% (1)	3% (3)	117
					Total Respondents	122

---

months. Sometimes, as in the case of an acquisition, the bank will accept the buyer's projected cash flows as the basis for the loan. From the lender's standpoint it is safer to lend money if the ratio of the amounted loan divided by the cash is low; it is riskier to lend if the ratio is high. When times are good and there is lots of money to lend and not enough people wanting to borrow, bankers are willing to take on more risk. They may lend 3.5 times the amount of projected cash flow. If the buyer is putting up half of the money, he may be able to pay 7.0 times cash flow for an attractive target. When money is tight and lenders are more risk averse, they may be willing to lend only 2.5 times the amount of cash flow. (They will also be fussier about using a projection.) If the buyer is coming up with half the money, he can pay only 5.0 times cash flow.

The ups and downs of credit availability are reflected in the market prices for companies. In 2004, a time that Fleet Capital noted as "the best time for mid-sized company acquisitions," Fleet reported that some acquisitions were priced at "7–9 times EBIDTA." Fleet further stated that debt financing was priced low and buyers could expect to put in equity of 30% of the deal price or less. This was said to translate to an expected return for investors from the "high teens to 20%," because "Buyers feel they can afford to pay more for a company to take advantage of improved financial performance and stock appreciation in the future."

You may be concluding that some buyers seem to value a deal on how much they can afford to pay, and I think that is correct in many cases. If the CEO really wants a target, once that target is in his sights the upper end of what the buyer will pay is based on what he can afford. The discounted cash-flow analysis will justify almost any price if you play with the assumptions long enough.

A target company can be valued in relation to its book value. Book value is an ancient accounting concept that is the basis of financial reporting. Assets are recorded on the "books" (the balance sheet) at the price originally paid for them. Some assets are revalued, or adjusted downward, in a systematic and rational way, such as periodic depreciation of fixed assets. Other assets are revalued based on loss estimates (the allowance for uncollectible receivables) or price indices (LIFO inventory). A more recent innovation is the periodic write-down for estimated impairment of goodwill. That term needs explaining.

From an accounting viewpoint, goodwill is the price paid in excess of book value of assets acquired. It is an intangible asset valued according to the advantage or reputation a business has acquired over and above its tangible assets. If the acquisitive distributor buys assets from another company and pays more than the book value, an asset called goodwill will appear on the buyer's balance sheet. Each year, the buyer's outside accountants will go through an exercise with management to determine if the goodwill has been impaired.

CEOs reported to me in my research for this study that they often pay more, sometimes much more, than book value for the businesses they acquire. This amount is the premium paid for the earning power of the business. I again refer you to the chapter on customer profitability analysis as a method for testing the value of a distribution business.

We have to consider risk in placing a value on premium for the purchase of a distribution business. Consider a popular way for buyers to reduce risk. If the seller is willing to accept payment for the premium on a contingency basis, the buyer will pay based only on the sales (or gross profit, or operating profit) he actually obtained from doing business with the seller's customers over a certain period of time. Even a conservative buyer might get comfortable with a hefty premium if it will be paid only out of actual profits from the acquired company.

It's easy enough for a seller to paint a rosy picture of how well the business will perform under the new owner. There may be many reasons why next year will be even better than this year: better economic conditions, new customers, new products, better margins, cost reductions, improved asset management. Asking the seller to put his money where his mouth is, to share the risk with the buyer, seems to be a reasonable way to reconcile the inevitable gap between the risk the buyer is willing to take and the demands made by the seller.

It is often said that a strategic buyer will pay more than a financial buyer for the same business. This comment deserves some thought, since acquisitive distributors are strategic buyers. The strategic buyer is going to add the acquired business to his existing enterprise. He analyzes prospective acquisitions in terms of the synergies offered: How can his existing company benefit from the acquisition? How can the acquired company benefit from becoming part of his existing business? There are usually opportunities to reduce operating costs, leverage suppliers and customers, enhance margins, etc. Buyers steadfastly argue that they are not about to pay the seller for the synergies they will enjoy, which, after all, are going to result from the buyer's internal efficiencies. Sellers are, of course, keenly aware of the thought process the strategic buyer is going through. An old real-estate saying goes, "A property is worth more to the guy next door." That logic applies when one distributor buys another; the projected synergies would most probably influence both the amount the seller wants and the price the buyer is willing to pay.

Evergreen Consulting conducts a simple analysis of the range of purchase prices a client is considering for a prospective acquisition. We develop a range of sales scenarios, ranging from very pessimistic to very optimistic, that the acquired company is likely to experience in the first 12 months following the acquisition. We then make a judgment about a conservative gross trading margin the company can expect, based on the target company's history and an analysis of its largest customers. Next we apply a conservative estimate of total operating expenses based on historical information, what we know about the company, and the way the buyer operates his own business. The litmus test for the various scenarios is the projected return on sales: Does it make sense? Where do we go from here? We evaluate the range of possible purchase prices, from what the buyer wants all the way down to the lowest price we had in mind. Each of the purchase prices is compared with the projected cash flow from the business, including the interest expense we expect to incur on financing the working capital needs of the acquired company. Our benchmarks are the cash return on our investment and the effect the acquisition will have on the value of our company.

Distribution is a risky business, with low barriers of entry and exit for competitors. Investors are entitled to a superior return on investment for risking their money. A patient investor could invest his money in a diversified portfolio of quality stocks and bonds and expect an 8%–11% compounded annual return over the years. He could invest in municipal bonds and enjoy tax-free returns and little risk, so the investment in distribution must pay a higher return.

The acquisitive distributor needs to keep his target return on investment in mind when pricing a prospective acquisition. My advice is to do some simple analytical work and determine a walk-away price, a line in the sand beyond which you will not go.

The price you present in your offer usually should not be the highest price you are willing to pay. Sellers expect that buyers hold back their top price until later in the negotiations, no matter how insistent the buyer is that his initial offer is "My highest and best offer—I'm not playing any games—take it or leave it." That gambit has been tried too many times already, and most sellers won't be convinced. I would suggest that the opening price be sensible enough to impress the buyer of your sincerity, to catch his interest, and to stimulate his imagination about what his personal financial picture would look like (and indeed how nice his life could be) if he sold the business to you.

I asked CEOs about the acquisitions they made that did not meet their expectations and what mistakes they made. Relatively few of the chief executives reported that their big mistake was that they overpaid.

If you are going after quality companies (not turnarounds)— the kind of businesses other buyers would like to buy, the type of company most likely to add to your bottom line and add value to your business—you have to be prepared to pay a fair price. My advice is that if you want to pay rock-bottom prices, you will have to go after distressed companies or wait patiently for those rare instances where you can "steal" someone else's business. I don't think that approach will result in a steady stream of successful deals.

Harvard Business Review comments, "Leaving some money on the table is OK if you realize that the most expensive deal is one that fails." Paying somewhat too much for the right company is far better than getting a great deal on the wrong one.

Letter of intent

After some back-and-forth discussions and compromises about the issues on the terms sheet, hopefully you and the seller will shake hands and put your initials on a revised terms sheet. Although it is not designed to be a binding contract, the terms sheet sketches out the major deal points and quickly leads to the letter of intent. In most cases the buyer's attorney will draft the letter of intent based on the terms sheet and the buyer's instructions. The seller's attorney will review the letter of intent for his client and will almost always suggest at least a couple changes, however minor. Lawyers usually need to prove that there is something wrong with the other lawyer's language, even if the document is fairly even-handed.

The letter of intent will almost always be non-binding on either party. The buyer will have the opportunity to get out of the deal if he doesn't like what he sees during due diligence. It is not customary to try to set parameters that would force the buyer to go ahead with the deal under certain conditions. The seller will also have the right to change his mind without any particular justification. He can just get cold feet and cancel the deal. The deal isn't complete until the closing, and the closing cannot happen until the parties agree on every detail of the definitive purchase agreement and a host of other documents. Failure to resolve any one of them can kill the deal, and the documents are usually not ready for signature until a few short hours (or minutes) before closing.

Sometimes major Wall Street deals include breakup fees, which one party must pay the other in case they don't go through with the deal. A breakup fee is analogous to a buyer's paying a seller for an option to buy a property for a certain period of time. The seller is compensated for temporarily taking his property off the market. A breakup fee is unusual in a smaller transaction. Such fees, even when they are used, are subject to disputes in which the parties blame one another for holding up the deal. Most sellers can't expect to demand a breakup fee in their letter of intent.

What is the purpose of a non-binding letter of intent? The letter of intent may go into more (or much more) detail about the price and terms of the transaction. The seller agrees not to enter into negotiations with other buyers, or at least to report activity with other buyers, for a certain period of time. This commitment gives the buyer some assurance about his costly and time-consuming investment in due diligence. The letter of intent gives the buyer a limited amount of time to complete his diligence and to have his attorney prepare a definitive purchase agreement and other documents, such as employment agreements and real-estate leases, if needed. The letter of intent will usually set a proposed closing date for the transaction, although the date is often postponed for a variety of reasons. A short delay in closing can, but does not usually, cause a deal to fall apart.

The transition from the negotiation phase to due diligence

Harvard Business Review recommends a "new mind-set" to help the negotiating team transition from dealmaker mentality to an implementation mind-set:

1. *Start with the end in mind.* Imagine the deal 12 months out: What has gone wrong? How do you know if it's a success? Who should have been involved earlier?

2. *Help them prepare, too.* Surprising the other side doesn't make sense, because if they promise things they can't deliver, you both lose.

3. *Treat alignment as a shared responsibility.* If your counterpart's interests aren't aligned, it's your problem, too.

4. *Send one message.* Brief implementation teams on both sides of the deal together so everyone has the same information.

5. *Manage negotiation like a business process.* Combine a disciplined preparation process with post-negotiation reviews.

CHAPTER SIX

Phase Three: Due Diligence

"Are we disposed to be among the number
of those who, having eyes, see not, and
having ears, hear not? For my part, whatever
anguish of spirit it may cost, I am willing
to know the whole truth; to know the worst,
and to provide for it."

Patrick Henry
• • • • • • • •

The premise underlying this book is that making small acquisitions is a good idea for distributors who want profitable growth. There is a strong body of evidence that most acquisitions don't meet the buyer's expectations. The purpose of the groundbreaking research that went into this report is to understand the reasons so many distributors are disappointed by their acquisitions.

Based on my own experiences and work with my clients, I started out with the notion that most acquisitive distributors don't a good job with due diligence and integration. Responses from CEOs validated these assumptions. (See Exhibit 6-1.)

Due diligence basics

According to *Venture Capital Glossary*:

> Due diligence is the process of investigation and evaluation, performed by investors, into the details of a potential investment, such as an examination of operations and management and the verification of material facts.

Due diligence is not a term everyone in the M&A world can agree on. *Computer World* defines the term as follows:

> Due diligence is the process of examining the financial underpinnings of a corporation as one of the first steps in a pending merger, equity investment, or large-scale IT purchase, with the goal of understanding the risks associated with the deal. Issues that could be reviewed

include corporate capitalization, material agreements, litigation history, public filings, intellectual property, and IT systems.

The due diligence required in a particular transaction depends on the attitude of the buyer and the business he intends to purchase. A good starting point is the target company's industry. The article in *Computer World* is about technology acquisitions. The due diligence needed to assess the risks of buying a technology company is obviously not the same as that for buying a chain of retail stores, an insurance company, or a distributor.

Those making the due diligence assessment for the acquirer are focused on risk. Howard Schilt, author of *Financial Shenanigans* (2002), talks about accounting gimmicks such as

- Early recognition of revenues.
- Recording revenues that are not genuine.
- Increasing income with a one-time gain.
- Shifting expenses to a later period.
- Failure to record or disclose all liabilities.
- Shifting income to a later period.
- Shifting expenses to the current period.

Not all of the risks relate to the financial statements. The risks, per an American Institute of CPAs statement on accounting standards, include management characteristics, industry conditions, and operating conditions. A thorough due diligence process consists of *business* due diligence as well as *financial* due diligence.

Tendency to focus on financial due diligence at the expense of other areas

The historical emphasis on due diligence is focused on financial data and, to a lesser extent, on legal issues. Much due diligence work is typically conducted by accounting personnel, and the tests are similar to the work done by auditors. The legal work is akin to what is done in a real-estate purchase: verify that

EXHIBIT 6-1.1

Lessons Learned from the *Most* Successful Acquisitions

Think of your company's most successful acquisition in the last 10 years, in terms of meeting company expectations for the deal. Please reflect on what was learned in terms of selecting the target, structuring the deal, due diligence and integration.

	Very Satisfied	Satisfied	Neither Satisfied nor Dissatisfied	Dissatisfied	Very Dissatisfied	Response Average
Looking back, how do you feel about the process you used for choosing the acquisition target	25% (29)	53% (62)	15% (17)	6% (7)	1% (1)	2.04
Looking back, how do you feel about the price paid, terms and deal structure for this acquisition	32% (37)	42% (49)	18% (21)	6% (7)	2% (2)	2.03
Looking back, how do you feel about the due diligence performed for this acquisition	22% (25)	41% (47)	16% (18)	21% (24)	2% (2)	2.41
Looking back, how do you feel about the way integration of this acquisition was handled	23% (26)	50% (57)	10% (11)	17% (19)	2% (2)	2.25
					Total Respondents	116

the seller has good title to the assets, that there are no unrecorded liens on the property, that the taxes have been paid.

Business operations have become so dependent on the integrity of information systems that a review of the IT function has become standard in most transactions. This is certainly true in the acquisition of a distributor, and failures in this area can be painful.

The intensity of litigation and potential liabilities for alleged bad employment practices, product defects, and environmental risk (to name only three) has stepped up the due diligence work in the area of legal exposure and insurance coverage.

In addition to the above generic risks, applicable to almost any industry, acquisitions of distributors pose a number of special problems. As a risk-averse business person, I advise clients to follow a detailed work plan for their due diligence.

EXHIBIT 6-1.2

Lessons Learned from the *Least* Successful Acquisitions

Think of your company's least successful acquisition in the last 10 years, in terms of failing to meet company expectations for the deal. Please reflect on what was learned in terms of selecting the target, structuring the deal, due diligence and integration.

	Very Satisfied	Satisfied	Neither Satisfied nor Dissatisfied	Dissatisfied	Very Dissatisfied	Response Average
Looking back, how do you feel about the strategic reasons for making this acquisition	13% (9)	48% (34)	27% (19)	8% (6)	4% (3)	2.44
Looking back, how do you feel about the price paid, terms and deal structure for this acquisition	6% (4)	33% (22)	33% (22)	19% (13)	9% (6)	2.93
Looking back, how do you feel about the due diligence performed for this acquisition	2% (1)	32% (21)	26% (17)	35% (23)	6% (4)	3.12
Looking back, how do you feel about the way integration of this acquisition was handled	3% (2)	28% (18)	25% (16)	26% (17)	18% (12)	3.29
					Total Respondents	71

The work is organized into the following areas:

- Accounting and finance.
- Sales and marketing.
- Customer profitability analysis.
- Management information systems.
- Operations and logistics.
- Human resources.
- Legal.

Exhibit 6-2.1 through 6-2.7 are an analysis of the due diligence work typically performed by acquisitive distributors in each of these areas.

EXHIBIT 6-2.1

Accounting & Finance

	Always	Usually	Sometimes	Rarely	Never	Response Total
1. Bank debt	39% (46)	37% (44)	17% (20)	4% (5)	3% (4)	119
2. Mezzanine financing	1% (1)	2% (2)	17% (14)	12% (10)	67% (54)	81
3. Venture capital	0% (0)	0% (0)	5% (4)	11% (9)	84% (69)	82
4. Private equity	12% (10)	14% (12)	15% (13)	6% (5)	53% (46)	86
5. Seller financing	8% (8)	21% (20)	33% (32)	8% (8)	29% (28)	96
6. Earn outs/contingent payments	14% (13)	15% (14)	39% (36)	4% (4)	28% (26)	93

Total Respondents | 121

EXHIBIT 6-2.2

Sales & Marketing

	Always	Usually	Sometimes	Rarely	Never	Response Total
1. Analyze customer profitability	53% (59)	23% (26)	14% (16)	5% (6)	4% (4)	111
2. Meet with customers	19% (20)	15% (16)	25% (27)	25% (26)	16% (17)	106
3. Review customer contracts	62% (68)	21% (23)	6% (6)	7% (8)	4% (4)	109

Total Respondents | 111

EXHIBIT 6-2.3

Suppliers

	Always	Usually	Sometimes	Rarely	Never	Response Total
1. Meet with suppliers	35% (39)	29% (32)	15% (16)	12% (13)	9% (10)	110
2. Review supplier agreements	70% (77)	15% (17)	7% (8)	2% (2)	5% (6)	110
					Total Respondents	111

EXHIBIT 6-2.4

Management Information Systems

	Always	Usually	Sometimes	Rarely	Never	Response Total
1. Interview systems management	50% (53)	23% (25)	11% (12)	6% (6)	10% (11)	107
2. Meet with systems vendors	17% (17)	16% (16)	24% (24)	22% (22)	23% (23)	102
3. Evaluate software contracts	42% (44)	24% (25)	15% (16)	5% (5)	14% (15)	105
4. Inspect equipment	55% (59)	28% (30)	10% (11)	3% (3)	5% (5)	108
					Total Respondents	109

EXHIBIT 6-2.5
Operations & Logistics

	Always	Usually	Sometimes	Rarely	Never	Response Total
1. Site visit all warehouses	85% (94)	11% (12)	2% (2)	0% (0)	2% (2)	110
2. Inspect delivery vehicles	53% (56)	19% (20)	12% (13)	8% (9)	8% (8)	106
3. Inspect warehouse equipment	59% (65)	22% (24)	13% (14)	4% (4)	3% (3)	110
					Total Respondents	110

EXHIBIT 6-2.6
Human Resources

	Always	Usually	Sometimes	Rarely	Never	Response Total
1. Interview managers	66% (73)	23% (25)	4% (4)	6% (7)	1% (1)	110
2. Interview sales people	52% (57)	28% (30)	5% (5)	10% (11)	6% (6)	109
3. Interview other employees	31% (34)	31% (34)	19% (21)	14% (15)	5% (6)	110
4. Review non-competition agreements	69% (75)	11% (12)	6% (7)	7% (8)	6% (7)	109
5. Review labor agreements	64% (69)	10% (11)	5% (5)	8% (9)	13% (14)	108
6. Review retirement plans	65% (72)	10% (11)	7% (8)	10% (11)	7% (8)	110
7. Review sales compensation plans	74% (81)	19% (21)	3% (3)	3% (3)	2% (2)	110
8. Review employee manuals & handbooks	56% (62)	20% (22)	8% (9)	9% (10)	7% (8)	111
					Total Respondents	112

EXHIBIT 6-2.7

Legal

	Always	Usually	Sometimes	Rarely	Never	Response Total
1. Evaluate environmental risks	73% (80)	13% (14)	6% (6)	4% (4)	5% (5)	109
2. Evaluate employment practices exposure	56% (61)	20% (22)	8% (9)	7% (8)	7% (8)	108
3. Evaluate product liability exposure	62% (65)	16% (17)	11% (12)	9% (9)	2% (2)	105
4. Evaluate retirement plan obligations	67% (72)	11% (12)	7% (7)	7% (8)	7% (8)	107
5. Analyze intellectual property	46% (48)	16% (17)	17% (18)	10% (10)	11% (11)	104
					Total Respondents	110

Desire to keep due diligence costs down by doing the work internally

It's imperative that acquisitive distributors not cut any corners in due diligence. It is cause for alarm when cost-conscious buyers resist doing their homework for cost reasons. It's tempting to have the acquirer's employees perform the due diligence work, mostly to save money. The typical person asked to do this work is the acquirer's controller or CFO. This individual should definitely be part of the due diligence team, but not necessarily the team leader. Some distributor financial people are great at their jobs but don't have any experience or training in doing due diligence work. Many controllers spent part of their careers in public accounting, possibly doing audits including purchase investigations, but they still may not see the big picture. Another problem with this approach is that it may become focused almost entirely on financial issues at the expense of other exposure areas of great importance.

A second reason for skipping part of the due diligence work is time pressures. The timetable for closing a deal can easily fall apart for a wide variety of reasons. The easiest way to get back on schedule is to rush the due diligence. Nothing could please the seller more. This can be a big mistake.

Another reason for cutting back on due diligence is caving in to resistance from the seller. If the seller is reluctant to let you perform reasonable due diligence procedures, I believe you should run, not walk, to the nearest exit.

Lack of experience in what to look for in due diligence

The acquisitive distributor needs to put together a cross-functional team of his best people to do a complete purchase investigation. If the deal goes through, the buyer is going to hold his people accountable for the successful integration of the acquired company.

The buyer's IS manager and his most capable IS expert (if it isn't the manager, which is often the case) must conduct a thorough review of the seller's information system. The buyer's most experienced sales executive needs to conduct a thorough investigation of the seller's sales function and interview the sales managers and the key salespeople. The buyer's operations expert must do a complete review of the seller's logistics and operations. Ditto for human resources and marketing. A qualified attorney must perform the legal review. I believe it is almost always a good idea to have the buyer's outside accounting firm play a role in the financial review, even if it is limited to an oversight function.

Difficulties posed by doing due diligence out of town or off site

Some sellers are obsessed with maintaining confidentiality during the due diligence process. They fear that word of the transaction will leak out if their people are aware of the proposed transaction. How can the buyer perform due diligence under such conditions? A possible solution is for the buyer to conduct the financial due diligence in the office of the seller's outside accounting firm. Much of the financial work can be done using the outside accountant's work papers, and many of the buyer's questions can be answered by the staff accountants who are familiar with their client's business. The seller's controller or CFO is almost always aware of the proposed transaction, and that person is able to respond to questions and provide additional documentation without arousing suspicion at his company. It would be difficult or nearly impossible to do a thorough financial review without cooperation from the seller's top financial person. In many cases, usually involving small companies, the owner-manager is also the CFO and has ready access to needed information.

Special due diligence issues with distributors

About 80% of distributor assets are receivables and inventories

Receivables and inventories are the major assets for most distributors, usually about 80% of total assets. Depending on turnover, these two assets may be similar in total value. Each raises valuation issues.

If the buyer is acquiring assets, accounts receivable risk can be minimized fairly easily. The buyer can exclude the receivables from the transaction altogether, leaving the job of collecting the money to the seller. This can create problems for both sides, however. Sending payments to two difference parties can be confusing to customers and may antagonize them. For a seamless transition, it isn't desirable for the buyer to keep reminding the customer of the change in ownership. The seller may find that some of his former customers try to delay payments or avoid paying altogether, taking advantage of the confusion and the former owner's lack of leverage in collecting his receivables.

Another option is to leave the receivables out of the transaction, but for the buyer to agree to accept payments from the customers and forward the funds (and supporting data) to the former owner. This approach is better for everyone: The customers don't have any extra hassles, the buyer presents a smooth transition to his customers, and the seller maximizes the money he is able to collect.

Inventories present a challenge in many wholesaler-distributor transactions. This asset is as much as 40% to 50% or more of the seller's balance sheet. Inevitably, some of the inventory is not saleable in the ordinary course of business. Depending on the seller's inventory method, the inventory may be carried on the books at an amount in excess of its value.

Jim Collins, author of *Good to Great*, says, "Imagine walking back into the warehouse and instead of seeing boxes of cereal and crates of apples, you see stacks and stacks of dollar bills... that's exactly how you should think of inventory."

One of the main causes of dead distributor inventory is product purchased for specific customers. This may be hard to spot because the products may have been purchased very recently. Distributors are notoriously bad at getting commitments from their customers for specially ordered products.

Another problem is ordering errors, including relying on historical sales patterns to replenish stock that regular users have simply stopped buying. This is also hard to spot, as the products may have been purchased in the recent past. Distributors depend on historical usage to project future usage when ordering inventory.

A wholesaler-distributor will occasionally get caught with inventory that his supplier superseded with a new product or a new packaging configuration, or possibly dropped from his line. This is also hard to identify, as the product may be fairly fresh.

A client once asked me to visit a company he had just acquired. The purpose of the visit was to assist with the integration by presenting a training program about financial topics. I asked for a tour prior to the meeting, part of which was a walk through the warehouse, where I saw something disturbing. Some of the boxes (described as "expensive stuff") were dirty and had the telltale sign of obsolescence: a number of stickers from physical inventory counts. Like the rings on the trunk of a fallen tree, each sticker meant the item was one year older. I called the CEO on my cell phone to inquire and found that the inventory due diligence had been done by accounting personnel, mostly by reviewing financial records. The dirty boxes with lots of stickers had apparently been placed in a back room during the site visit. Unfortunately for the buyer, he had purchased quite a bit of expensive but obsolete inventory.

Trade payables

Other than bank debt, most of the distributor's liabilities are accounts payable to product vendors. These have to be looked at carefully due to the high level of transaction volume and the existence of claims and counterclaims.

Many supplier product lines are invoiced to the distributor at list price. In order to support sales to large end users, the suppliers may offer a program to provide discounted prices for sales to the selected customers. To claim the discounts, the distributor is required to provide some form of proof of sales to the selected customers. The supplier will then issue a credit memo, or simply allow the distributor to deduct the amount due from a remittance. Disputes may arise due to differences in timing, misunderstandings about the customers, and products that qualify for support, price increases and decreases, and other reasons.

These distributor-vendor disputes can simmer for months or years, or even go undetected for extended periods, due to the transaction volumes. Even if the buyer does not assume the trade debt, a subsequent dispute with a key supplier may be hard to resolve without alienating the vendor.

It is a good idea to review the vendors' most recent monthly statements and to try to confirm the amounts due.

> ## True story
>
> The buyer was thrilled to acquire a truck dealership with a big stock of new equipment. The deal was a stretch for the acquirer, who had plans for major sales growth. The optimism was based on the seller's sales projections and analysis of the market.
>
> The buyer later found a glut of new truck inventory on the market and heavy discounting, resulting in a painful loss of inventory value. The buyer was not up to date on market conditions in this potentially disastrous purchase.
>
> **Advice to buyers:** Do your own homework. Don't rely on the seller's assessment of market conditions.

Rebate claims from marketing/buying groups

Distributor buying or marketing groups have formed in many lines of trade. The primary objective of most of these groups is to leverage the distributors' volume to make better deals with suppliers. In most cases, the groups are the independent distributors' effort to remain competitive with large national distributors or consolidators.

The typical program provides a promotional allowance based on the volume of purchases of qualifying products from the suppliers. The buying group collects the funds from the participating suppliers and passes the proceeds (or most of the proceeds) on to the distributors who earned the allowances through their purchasing volume. The promotional allowances are often processed two or three months in arrears due to the processing time needed for checks and balances, and for the funds to pass through so many hands.

The promotional allowances are difficult to audit due to the transaction volume, timing, varying qualifications to participate, etc. The dollars involved are significant, but most distributors don't accrue them or do a good job keeping track of what is owed them.

It's wise to review the details of these programs, examine recent activity, and confirm amounts with the buying/marketing groups.

Sheltered income programs with customers

Depending on the line of trade, some distributors have entered into rebate programs with their customers. They are typically based on volume purchased, paid quarterly, and may involve large amounts. Most distributors do not accrue these amounts, so they could be an unrecorded liability. A review of recent activity and contracts with large customers should uncover the existence of these arrangements and enable an estimate of the obligations.

Consignment inventories

Consigned inventories can involve both customers and suppliers. Distributor-owned inventory at customer locations has become more popular in recent years. The products tend to be slow moving; dead inventory is common. Care needs to be taken to verify ownership of inventory at remote locations and to be sure it is insured.

Sales taxes

Distributors have an ongoing exposure to sales tax audits by state and local authorities. Most distributors do not collect sales taxes from their customers based on exemptions such as purchase for resale, purchase for use in manufacturing, direct pay permits, or purchase by a non-profit. Some distributors are notoriously poor in keeping their records current with valid exemption certificates, or in taking care to be sure the proper amount of sales tax is collected based on the jurisdiction or product, or in collecting taxes for shipments to other states.

State tax agencies know this, and in their search for cash they sometimes initiate sales tax audits aimed at distributors. The audits can be very time-consuming, and states sometimes test a small block of transactions and propose a settlement going back three years. This special area of contingent liability must be explored and quantified.

Outside salespeople and non-competition agreements

Sales compensation is the largest operating expense for most distributors. Outside salespeople, often about one-third of the total employees, may earn one-half of the company's total compensation.

The special skills possessed by top outside salespeople are precious and well rewarded by distributors. Many distributors protect these critical business assets (not on the balance sheet, but assets nonetheless) by using non-competition agreements. The use of such agreements may extend to other employees in customer-sensitive positions. I am a strong advocate for non-competition agreements. When used properly, these can provide a powerful extra degree of security for both the company and its employees.

Acquirers who recognize the value of these agreements need to take steps to determine if they are legally binding for the buyer, and also to see that the company has copies of the necessary documents on file for each employee in question. The acquirer and his legal counsel need to evaluate the way the company has managed the employment agreements, including how apparent violations were handled. The buyer may be interested to know if the company respects the employment agreements between other companies and their employees.

Commission plans

It is not uncommon for an outside salesperson to be the highest-paid person in a distribution business. Many distribution executives, including owner-managers, accept the possibility that one or more of their superstar salespeople may earn commission income that exceeds the amount paid to top executives. The enlightened ones are pleased by this phenomenon. If the sales compensation plan works properly, the highest-paid salespeople maintain customer relationships that generate operating profits, which drive the company's success (including the bonuses paid to the managers themselves).

Acquirers need to understand the mechanics of the sales compensation plan and how it is administered. Some distributors make special deals with key salespeople. These deals, secret or otherwise, can be troublesome. They are demoralizing to the staff and often divisive. Their existence may lead to demands for similar treatment by other members of the staff. Finally, an attempt by the buyer to rectify the disparity may result in the loss of key people and customers.

Customer profitability analysis

Customer profitability analysis (CPA) can be a one of the acquirer's most valuable tools for due diligence. Customer concentration is always a concern in distributor acquisitions. Most acquirers are fearful of paying a premium for a distributor whose profitability could be imperiled through the loss of one or two major customers. CPA uncovers customer concentration at the operating profit level, where it really counts. More traditional analysis at the sales or gross profit levels does not provide the needed information.

Ranking the target company's customers based on operating profit will uncover the relatively small number of customer relationships from which the company derives most of its operating profit. These are the customers who must be protected at all costs.

Salesperson concentration is also a major concern for acquirers. CPA reveals the handful of salespeople who maintain the company's most profitable customer relationships.

The acquirer is purchasing a stream of future cash flows from the target's most profitable customer relationships. The buyer may be paying a significant premium for these relationships. Even the most thorough due diligence has time and budget constraints that prevent a close examination of every detail of the target company. CPA enables the due diligence team to focus its efforts on the most critical elements of value.

Non-transferability of franchises and other vendor commitments

The acquirer must recognize the risk of losing critical product lines after the purchase, or possibly losing "most favored" status with a key supplier.

- Suppliers may have cancellation options triggered by a change of ownership. It may be necessary to be reappointed as distributor for some product lines.

- Suppliers often give "most favored distributor" status to some of their distributors. Loss of this status or a shift of support to a competitor can seriously reduce the value of a supplier product line.

- Another possibility is appointment of competitive distributors when a supplier loses confidence in one of its current distributors.

- Suppliers may take advantage of the change of ownership to resolve potential conflicts with other national, regional, and supplier-owned distributors.

- Suppliers may express respect for their relationship with a long-term loyal distributor by resisting the urge to sell direct to the distributor's end-user accounts. This loyalty may change due to a change of ownership.

A shrewd acquirer would be wise to establish a relationship with key suppliers before the closing, in addition to examining the details of the current arrangement including the franchise agreement (if any). The risks can be reduced by mutual assurances and also by a commitment to at least consider investing in expanding the relationship with the supplier.

Low barriers of entry and exit

The acquisitive distributor must assess the competition in the target company's markets during the strategic assessment phase. The acquisition itself may cause a change in the competitive landscape.

- One or more target company salespeople may be tempted to start their own business (often with support from a supplier).

- One or more of the salespeople may be lured away to a competitor, possibly to establish a new location in the market.

The acquirer would be smart to establish relationships with key employees prior to the closing. The buyer should be able to assess the employees' attitude toward the change of ownership and their reaction to the way he intends to run the business. Potentially serious cultural problems should be identifiable during the due diligence phase.

Labor union issues

Acquirers who are unfamiliar with operating a business with a labor union should approach unionized target companies with care. A tradition of adversarial relationships between employees and management is very difficult to change. Management can be frustrated by labor agreements that contain work rules and other restrictions on management's ability to make needed changes.

MIS compatibility issues

Most distributors are wedded to their information systems. Aside from the overreaction to the Y2K scare, it has been a long time since many wholesaler-distributors considered major upgrades to their systems. This is especially true if they were even thinking of selling the company.

- The good news is that the systems may fit comfortably, like a favorite pair of old shoes. The distributor staff is proficient at using the system.

- The bad news is that older systems often don't communicate well with trading partners (e-commerce) and cannot meet the changing needs of the business. They also don't communicate well with the buyer's system.

- The buyer may be faced with a large investment in hardware, software, system modifications, data conversion, and training. New systems are a major distraction for all employees, can cause an inward (slow growth) mentality, and may disrupt customer relationships.

It's great to buy a distributor with a state-of-the-art information system and a group of highly trained employees who know how to get the most out of the system. It is also very unusual.

Real-estate issues

Most distributors don't like to carry "brick and mortar" on the balance sheet. Real-estate ownership ties up valuable capital that can be better deployed by investing in receivables and inventory. The space needs of distributors can change rapidly, and the type of space distributors need is readily available in most markets.

Many owner-managers (or their family members) own the property the business uses outside the company. The lease rate may or not be at market price, and it is customary for the arrangement to be "triple net": the business pays all of the operating and ownership expenses, including insurance, maintenance, and taxes.

Resolving real-estate issues can be the key to the deal, especially in purchases from owner-managers. The cash flow from the real estate may be of vital importance to the family members who don't draw salaries from the business itself.

The real estate may actually be a critical factor, or even the catalyst, for the transaction. This is especially true when the family is saddled with an old building (possibly with environmental problems) in an aging industrial area. Continued rental income, or an outright sale of the building in the deal, may be of greatest importance to the seller.

Personal seat licenses/tickets/luxury boxes

Season tickets to sporting events can take on an importance far out of proportion to their innocent appearance. Some distributors do quite a bit of business entertaining, and sporting events are a popular way to spend time with customers and suppliers. Sometimes the tickets are used just as way of thanking trading partners and employees. And of course the tickets are sometimes used for personal or family enjoyment.

The right to purchase tickets, personal seat licenses, and luxury boxes may not be registered in the name of the company. You will have to be sure that the seller has not taken steps to switch the ownership to his own or someone else's name prior to closing the transaction, if it is important to you to continue having the tickets available. Team management can be very rigid about ownership transfers due to a history of disputes including litigation.

I know of at least one buyer who was furious when he found that ticket ownership didn't go with the business. Although the rights to the tickets were not included in the purchase agreement, the buyer assumed that this asset (not listed on the balance sheet) was included in the deal.

You may find the same concerns about club memberships that appear to be owned by the business. If you are counting on using the clubs, check it out.

Special due diligence issues with owner-managed businesses

I once heard a buyer describe the upcoming due diligence process to the owner-manager of a distributor he was buying. He said that due diligence was "worse than being examined with a proctoscope." The acquisitive distributor with good bedside manner can make the due diligence, however rigorous, less unpleasant.

Mixture of personal and business lives

Most owner-managers have their business and personal lives hopelessly entangled. Due diligence is going to discover lots of personal information about most owner-managers. They tend to be fiercely independent, private people in the first place. Owner-managers don't like to have strangers going through their life insurance policies, retirement investments, country club bills, tax returns, and legal documents, to name a few.

Secrecy

There are several schools of thought on the need for secrecy and the importance of keeping a prospective sale under wraps until the deal is closed.

There are some good reasons for wanting the keep the deal quiet. A pending transaction is distracting for the seller's employees. They may become very worried about their job security; some may decide to look for other employment right away. The most sensitive group may be the outside salespeople, some of whom may feel threatened. Competitors may try to hire away some of the company's outside salespeople during this period of instability. The seller's suppliers may be uncomfortable with the prospective buyer due to competing lines or other issues. The suppliers may feel compelled to look for additional distribution, and the seller's competitors may approach them. Even though the sale is not a direct threat to customers, competitors may cause a disruption in the marketplace by spreading rumors or by becoming more active. Finally, the owner-manager may not want anyone to know about the proposed transaction due to embarrassment in the event it falls through. From that point on, his employees will be suspicious that the business is for sale.

There are also some good reasons to be open concerning the possibility of a transaction. There have been so many mergers and acquisitions (in distribution and every other field) in recent years that deals have almost become non-events. Employees are fairly sophisticated; they are almost surprised to think that selling has never crossed the owner's mind. If the company is known to be successful, employees might well wonder why no one has tempted the owner with an attractive offer.

There is a major risk in trying to keep the deal a secret until the last possible minute. If the owner-manager chooses not to tell his people, and they find out from someone else, there is a major breach of trust. Unfortunately, word of pending distributor transactions usually leaks out. Buyers want to talk with suppliers during the due diligence process. This step can be critical when supplier approval is needed to transfer a product line or franchise. Most franchise agreements are not transferable without the supplier's approval, and successful transition may be a contingency in the deal. Supplier personnel who find out about a pending transaction are often guilty of spreading the word throughout their own organization and, in turn, to other distributors. Another common source of leaks is a large distributor who is purchasing a smaller one. The feasibility study in the buyer's organization, or due diligence, spreads the word around the industry quickly.

When weighing the pros and the cons, in most cases I advise the seller to be as open as possible with his people. He can carefully plan what he is going to say and can tailor his message to the individuals he is talking to. He can have a one-to-one conversation with anyone he chooses. In many cases the CFO and one or two trusted senior people may be part of the process from the very beginning. The senior management team should be told first, followed by the outside sales team and then the support staff. These discussions are usually held just prior to the due diligence, when the chance of word getting out is greatest.

Transactions and business relationships between the family and the business

There may be a variety of transactions and business relationships between the family and the business, such as real-estate leases, salaries and bonuses, loans and advances, consulting agreements, deferred compensation agreements, retirement plan contributions, company-provided vehicles, cell phones, computers and software, life insurance policies, and even furnishings and art objects. Family members may provide services to the business, and the business may provide services to the family members (such as the company accountants preparing tax returns, company lawyers providing legal services, family members not paying for company products, etc.).

Some of these relationships were probably explained in the add-backs and adjustments phase of determining the purchase price, especially where the seller might feel that the relationship is not on an arm's-length basis. Due diligence in this area must be done with care. The relationships may be hard to detect and sensitive (one family member's benefiting at the expense of others). Some of the transactions may be improper and have negative tax implications. The buyer does want to know what expenses will not be recurring, and does not want to assume any of the sellers' tax liabilities.

Validation of assumptions and projections underlying the valuation model

The chapter about deal structuring includes comments on valuation and the discounted cash-flow models often used to validate the price to be paid for the business. Critical assumptions about the business underlie the computations used in these models, starting with the historical financial information provided by the seller.

The buyer relies on the seller's representations when formulating the offer, and he must validate all of those representations during the due diligence process. The financial due diligence should be performed first, mostly to assure the buyer that the seller's information is reliable. If discrepancies arise, the buyer may want to revise his offer or cancel the deal entirely.

Weight placed on recent events including subsequent developments

I believe it is usually in the seller's favor to get the due diligence done quickly and to close the deal as soon as possible. It is often in the buyer's best interests to be patient and not rush the transaction to closing. I'm not saying that the buyer should drag his feet, deliberately stretching the timeline so that the deal doesn't close on schedule. That would be an act of bad faith. The seller may be worried, and justifiably so, that an extended period of waiting time decreases the chances of maintaining secrecy.

The reason for scheduling a reasonable amount of time between the letter of intent and the closing and not moving to speed it up is to enable the buyer to see how the seller's representations about the future actually unfold. The buyer should carefully weigh the importance of events following the letter of intent: customers gained and lost, sales and margin trends, employee problems, issues with suppliers, etc. Some of these events may be seen as so significant that they are grounds for renegotiating the deal or calling it off.

There may be risks to the buyer for waiting. The subsequent events may be positive enough for the seller to cause him to demand a better deal or change his mind about selling. Another buyer may enter the scene and steal the deal. These factors need to be weighed in each case.

Letter of intent changes

Buyers sometimes assure sellers that they have no plans to change the basic deal outlined in the letter of intent. Signing the letter of intent with a "high ball" offer, with definite plans to revise it downward during or after due diligence, is an act of bad faith.

Through due diligence, buyers often find reasons to ask the seller to change the deal agreed to in the letter of intent. The reasons sometimes have to do with the buyer's ability to obtain financing for the deal. The buyer needs to be prepared to justify proposed changes, and the seller must to be willing to listen. This can be a delicate stage in the transaction process. It is not at all unusual for buyers to try to renegotiate, and it is not uncommon for deals to fall apart at this point.

Definitive purchase agreement

The buyer's attorney or the seller's attorney may prepare the first draft of the purchase agreement. There will probably be many revisions by the time the final agreement is signed. Most buyers prefer to wait until most or all of the due diligence is complete before they start spending money on legal fees for the purchase agreement and other documents. The legal work is costly, so the buyer wants to be confident the deal will go through before the lawyer's clock starts running.

According to *Harvard Business Review*, "Signing a contract is the beginning of a process of creating value...the real challenge is designing a deal that works in practice...a signed contract represents a commitment to work together to create value."

Warranties and representations, baskets, and caps

Depending on the way the purchase is structured, especially if the buyer is purchasing stock or real estate, the purchase agreement will include significant warranties and representations from the seller to the buyer. These provisions are unfamiliar territory to many sellers. Some agreements include baskets and caps, which set minimum amounts of losses before the buyer can make a claim and serve as limitations on the seller's total liability.

Employment agreements including non-competes

The buyer's attorneys will probably prepare the first draft of any employment agreements. The typical letter of intent does not go into much detail about the employment agreements, so there may be much for the lawyers to talk about. The seller's commitment not to compete with the buyer, not to solicit employees, etc., is sometimes included in the employment agreement and may be in the purchase agreement. These important details are sometimes a source of friction in the future; therefore, they must be given appropriate attention.

Closing checklist

There are many obstacles to getting to the closing table. The many parties involved in the transaction don't want it to fail due to a minor detail. A closing checklist will help to prevent an oversight. The buyer and seller each need to maintain a to-do list of everything to be completed before the closing. Both the buyer and the seller are dependent on outside parties to provide signatures, documents, releases, account numbers, and other items. They may have no sense of urgency about getting those things done on time.

Delays, last-minute problems, wire transfers, closing process

The tension surrounding a closing is sometimes due to circumstances beyond the control of the people in the room. Wire transfers sometimes fail to go through, documents have major errors, and banks make mistakes. People can get nervous when they have planes to catch. The acquisitive distributor needs to remain focused and in control.

Post-closing negotiations and claims

You can't provide for every contingency or anticipate all of the things that may happen after the purchase is closed. The buyer and seller often have claims against one another in the months (or years) following. The acquisitive distributor has to expect the possibility of filing a claim or defending a claim. It's part of the game.

Due diligence: deal killer?

Lessons from the Master Acquirers states, "A deal that dies at the due diligence stage almost always dies for the right reasons... acquirers have wiped more value off their market capitalization through failures in due diligence than through lapses on any other part of the deal process."

The *Harvard Business Review* article "When to Walk Away from a Deal" (April 2004) poses four due diligence questions:

1. What are we buying?
2. What is the target's stand-alone value?
3. Where are the synergies and skeletons?
4. What's our walk-away price?

Lessons from the Master Acquirers warns, "Do not let the thrill of the chase get the testosterone flowing." There are "two common arguments for ignoring the numbers":

1. This deal is the last of its kind.
2. If we don't buy it, one of our competitors will.

The book points out that "It's probably better to let the competition overpay than you...doubtless there are deals that should happen for strategic reasons even when the numbers don't sound promising, but they are few and far between." As the old saying goes, sometimes the best deals are the ones that don't get made.

Use of outside advisors

The world's greatest heart surgeon wouldn't try to operate on himself. The world's greatest golfers take golf lessons. Warren Buffett uses outside advisors. Enough said.

Exhibit 6-3 shows how acquisitive distributors use outside advisors.

EXHIBIT 6-3

Use of Outside Advisors

	Always	Usually	Sometimes	Rarely	Never	Response Total
Attorneys						
1. Strategizing	32% (24)	11% (8)	11% (8)	17% (13)	30% (23)	76
2. Identifying targets	2% (1)	5% (3)	8% (5)	20% (13)	66% (43)	65
3. Contacting Targets	0% (0)	9% (6)	18% (12)	18% (12)	54% (35)	65
4. Valuation	13% (9)	13% (9)	15% (10)	19% (13)	39% (26)	67
5. Negotiations with targets	28% (19)	16% (11)	28% (19)	14% (10)	14% (10)	69
6. Finding lenders	0% (0)	3% (2)	16% (10)	17% (11)	63% (40)	63
7. Negotiating with lenders	20% (13)	6% (4)	8% (5)	12% (8)	54% (35)	65
8. Drafting agreements	94% (77)	4% (3)	1% (1)	0% (0)	1% (1)	82
9. Due diligence	47% (35)	31% (23)	13% (10)	4% (3)	5% (4)	75
10. Integration	5% (3)	5% (3)	14% (9)	36% (24)	41% (27)	66
Accountants						
1. Strategizing	41% (30)	23% (17)	18% (13)	12% (9)	7% (5)	74
2. Identifying targets	5% (3)	6% (4)	23% (15)	20% (13)	46% (30)	65
3. Contacting Targets	2% (1)	6% (4)	10% (6)	25% (16)	57% (36)	63
4. Valuation	59% (48)	11% (9)	16% (13)	9% (7)	5% (4)	81
5. Negotiations with targets	13% (9)	10% (7)	30% (20)	18% (12)	28% (19)	67
6. Finding lenders	8% (6)	17% (12)	30% (21)	13% (9)	32% (23)	71
7. Negotiating with lenders	21% (15)	8% (6)	30% (21)	10% (7)	31% (22)	71
8. Drafting agreements	28% (19)	19% (13)	23% (16)	13% (9)	17% (12)	69
9. Due diligence	67% (52)	15% (12)	10% (8)	3% (2)	5% (4)	78
10. Integration	18% (13)	17% (12)	25% (18)	15% (11)	24% (17)	71
Investment Bankers						
1. Strategizing	19% (11)	18% (10)	37% (21)	12% (7)	14% (8)	57
2. Identifying targets	5% (3)	6% (4)	25% (16)	13% (8)	51% (32)	63
3. Contacting Targets	0% (0)	0% (0)	25% (15)	20% (12)	56% (34)	61
4. Valuation	8% (5)	9% (6)	27% (17)	16% (10)	41% (26)	64
5. Negotiations with targets	3% (2)	3% (2)	15% (9)	20% (12)	58% (35)	60
6. Finding lenders	11% (7)	11% (7)	14% (9)	11% (7)	54% (35)	65
7. Negotiating with lenders	8% (5)	8% (5)	10% (6)	10% (6)	65% (40)	62
8. Drafting agreements	5% (3)	3% (2)	10% (6)	15% (9)	67% (41)	61
9. Due diligence	5% (3)	5% (3)	8% (5)	18% (11)	64% (39)	61
10. Integration	2% (1)	2% (1)	7% (4)	18% (11)	72% (43)	60

EXHIBIT 6-3 *continued*

Use of Outside Advisors

	Always	Usually	Sometimes	Rarely	Never	Response Total
Other Advisors						
1. Strategizing	19% (11)	18% (10)	37% (21)	12% (7)	14% (8)	57
2. Identifying targets	11% (6)	20% (11)	48% (27)	7% (4)	14% (8)	56
3. Contacting Targets	5% (3)	7% (4)	41% (23)	11% (6)	36% (20)	56
4. Valuation	14% (8)	9% (5)	26% (15)	11% (6)	40% (23)	57
5. Negotiations with targets	11% (6)	4% (2)	24% (13)	17% (9)	44% (24)	54
6. Finding lenders	8% (4)	6% (3)	10% (5)	17% (9)	60% (31)	52
7. Negotiating with lenders	10% (5)	2% (1)	15% (8)	8% (4)	65% (34)	52
8. Drafting agreements	12% (6)	2% (1)	13% (7)	10% (5)	63% (33)	52
9. Due diligence	25% (14)	5% (3)	25% (14)	9% (5)	36% (20)	56
10. Integration	16% (9)	11% (6)	28% (16)	7% (4)	39% (22)	57

Total Respondents	91

CHAPTER SEVEN

Phase Four: Integration

"Productivity falls in less than an hour. People start thinking about themselves. Move fast and get the right people in place."

Dennis Kozlowski
• • • • • • • • • •

I started this project knowing that most distributor acquisitions disappoint the buyer. My theory was that the acquirers' biggest mistakes—the fatal errors, if you will—are in the due diligence and integration phases. Based on the input of over 400 battle-scarred distributor CEOs, I haven't changed my mind.

All of us have heard stories about how new owners ruin the great distribution companies they buy. The problem is that the sellers themselves are often the ones telling tales of how the buyer screwed up their company. Perhaps some of those stories are a matter of sour grapes, or maybe some of those companies were already in decline.

I've tried to set the record straight by asking buyers to talk about their integration techniques, to find out what works and what doesn't in this critical area. My overall conclusion is that bad integration can ruin a good deal. Even if everything else— good acquisition strategy, solid deal structure, effective due diligence—is done right, clumsy integration can be fatal. A good integration program may overcome mistakes made in the other phases of the acquisition process.

The art of M&A integration

From the viewpoint of the acquisitive distributor, integration is the process of making the newly acquired company part of the buying company. Buyers have totally different philosophies about how distributor integration should be done, ranging from one extreme to the other. Some believe in leaving the acquired company totally alone, letting it run autonomously so long as the results are acceptable. Others expunge the old identity of the acquired company immediately, plugging in their own management team and erasing all remnants of the old culture.

U.S. Filter made a series of acquisitions in the distribution business in the 1980s. It supposedly had a signage company waiting at the acquired company locations, in position to put up the U.S. Filter sign as soon as the ink dried at the closing. Alco-Standard, the old conglomerate, bought numerous distributors in the '70s and '80s. Alco was known as "the Corporate Partnership," leaving the company names, management teams, and cultures in place for many years (as long as the results were good).

Integration as a process

The value of a distribution business lies in its customer relationships. A chapter in this book is devoted to the subject of identifying the high-profit customers that generate the bulk of the operating profit and the people who control those relationships. Let me say that again: The value of a distribution business lies in its customer relationships.

Keep your finger off the trigger. Your job is to hold on to the people who control those relationships, and hang on to those customers. You need to keep them working toward the goals you set for the business you acquired. Yes, you may determine, after honest and reasonably patient effort, that some of those people can't or won't work toward your goals.

Don't stop the momentum of the business during integration (Jim Collins calls it the "flywheel" in his wonderful book *Good to Great*). It's very difficult, expensive, and time consuming to regain momentum in the marketplace. You want to build momentum, not stall it. Here is a simple plan:

- Start the integration process before the deal closes.
- Assign one of your people, hopefully on a full-time basis, to be the integration manager.
- If you will need to restructure the acquisition, don't wait too long.
- The culture fit of the acquisition is as important as exploiting the business opportunities.

Starting integration before the deal closes

I believe that you as the buyer should meet with the key people at the seller's company before the deal closes. This can be tricky, because many sellers will resist.

Years ago there was a "bottom-fisher" in the foodservice distribution business on the East Coast. He liked to buy distributors whom he knew were in dire financial straits. The principals in these companies and the buyer knew one another, and he would take advantage of the opportunity to meet privately with their top salespeople. Apparently, this was a mistake on the part of some of the sellers. The prospective buyer supposedly told the owners that he was offering only a discount on the book value of their companies. He had already talked with their sales reps and was prepared to hire them if the owner didn't want to sell. Why should he pay a premium, or even book value, if he could get the sales reps and the customers for free? If this is true, it may have been a bluff. But the desperate sellers were intimidated and deals were made.

Organize a series of small meetings, shortly before the closing, with each key employee. The meetings include the seller and the buyer, assuming the seller wants to participate (and he should). The meetings can accomplish the following:

- The buyer tells his story, his goals for the company, and how he wants to accomplish them.
- The key employee asks questions and (hopefully) gets comfortable with the buyer.
- The buyer has an opportunity (hopefully) to get comfortable with the key employee.

Paraphrasing Collins's comments in *Good to Great*, the buyer wants the key employees, and eventually all of the employees, to "see and feel the buildup of momentum." If they see a simple plan and a dedicated, selfless leader, there is a good chance they will overcome their concerns about the change of ownership. The buyer wants them to say, "That'll work, count me in." If the key employees buy in, word gets around fast.

As stated previously, I'm a big believer in non-competition agreements in distribution. This is a delicate subject requiring legal advice, as there are certainly many pitfalls, including the fact that agreements must be written with care and are not enforceable in some areas.

If the buyer feels strongly about the need for such agreements with key employees, and I believe in some cases he should, the entire deal may hinge on the seller's ability to deliver acceptable binding contracts at the time of closing. Successful meetings with the key employees prior to closing may be very helpful to the seller in getting the job done.

Integration planning

The ideal person to head the integration effort is one who was part of the team that put together the projections for the deal. It helps if the guy who signed off on the projections is responsible for making the deal work. Accountability goes a long way.

Exhibit 7-1 lists some of the integration tasks the acquisitive distributor performs.

Certain major integration tasks can be completed shortly before or shortly after the closing. Examples include meeting with key employees and executing employment agreements with them. Others can be staged before the closing, ready to be implemented without delay. For example, letters to trading partners can be prepared, addressed, and readied for mailing. Press releases can be drafted, meetings can be organized and rehearsed, etc. Some of the time-consuming work, such as preparation of employee handbooks, consolidation of fringe benefit plans, banking arrangements, and linkage of information systems can be done prior to closing.

Speed of integration

The time between closing and integration needs to be kept as short as possible. You need every chance you can get to demonstrate to employees and customers that the acquisition will work.

On the subject of rapid integration, a 1992 study by the accounting firm Coopers & Lybrand (now part of PricewaterhouseCoopers) recommended a 100-day target for the entire integration process. It noted, "The longer the acquirer waits to add value to the unit—presumably through some form of integration—the more expensive it will be to repay the premium paid to purchase the unit." Fair enough. A 1987 McKinsey & Co. study of 116 acquisitions concluded, "The chief culprit of integration was a slow pace."

EXHIBIT 7-1

Integration Tasks

	Important	Neither Important nor Unimportant	Unimportant	Not Sure	Response Total
		Importance			
1. Offer retention bonuses to selected employees	45% (41)	35% (32)	13% (12)	7% (6)	91
2. Revise sales commission plans	67% (61)	20% (18)	8% (7)	5% (5)	91
3. Obtain non-competition agreements from selected employees	59% (53)	18% (16)	20% (18)	3% (3)	90
4. Change company name	42% (37)	28% (25)	23% (20)	7% (6)	88
5. Send publicity releases	70% (62)	16% (14)	12% (11)	2% (2)	89
6. Replace signage on buildings and trucks	51% (44)	33% (28)	12% (10)	5% (4)	86
7. Send announcement to customers	92% (82)	3% (3)	4% (4)	0% (0)	89
8. Meet with buyers at key customers	85% (75)	9% (8)	5% (4)	1% (1)	88
9. Meet with key customer executives	83% (72)	11% (10)	3% (3)	2% (2)	87
10. Meet with sales staff one-to-one	94% (83)	6% (5)	0% (0)	0% (0)	88
11. Change fringe benefit programs	63% (54)	31% (27)	2% (2)	3% (3)	86
12. Meet with sales reps from key suppliers	65% (58)	24% (21)	10% (9)	1% (1)	89
13. Meet with key supplier executives	67% (58)	18% (16)	13% (11)	2% (2)	87
14. Issue new employee handbook; policy & procedures manual	77% (67)	16% (14)	3% (3)	3% (3)	87
15. Replace CEO	36% (29)	25% (20)	9% (7)	30% (24)	80
16. Replace CFO	45% (36)	24% (19)	6% (5)	25% (20)	80
17. Integrate back office functions	91% (79)	6% (5)	1% (1)	2% (2)	87
18. Integrate warehouse locations	76% (65)	14% (12)	5% (4)	5% (4)	85
19. Meet with employees in small groups	87% (76)	7% (6)	5% (4)	1% (1)	87
20. Hold company-wide employee meeting	85% (73)	10% (9)	2% (2)	2% (2)	86
21. Meet with employees one-to-one	81% (71)	15% (13)	2% (2)	2% (2)	88
				Total Respondents	97

Jim Collins writes in *Good to Great* about Darwin Smith, CEO of Kimberly-Clark (1971-1991) who transformed his company from papermaker to international consumer products giant. Smith "didn't change the direction of the company overnight, he evolved it over time. The transition wasn't like night and day." (Interesting comment, considering his name was Darwin.)

Exhibit 7-2 shows the timetable acquisitive distributor CEOs follow in their integration programs.

True story

A large sanitary supplies distributor acquired a good-sized company to expand geographically and add new product lines. After the closing, the buyer found that the acquired business operated in an entirely different way than his existing company.

He wanted to align the acquired business with his established practices but found it to be very difficult for two major reasons. First, the acquired company was far away from the main business. Second, the existing company was not that much larger than the business it acquired. He did not have the manpower needed to replace people at the acquired company.

It was necessary to work problems out patiently and from a long distance. This process took much longer than expected.

Advice to buyers: The buyer was still working out people problems five years after the purchase. People have trouble making a big cultural shift. Plan the needed changes and address them up front, before the closing. Put everything on the table immediately: salaries, benefits, results expected, even work hours.

The acquisitive distributor should try to resist making too many changes, but the changes you do make are best done as quickly as possible. Avoid what Collins calls the "flip-flop" strategy of integration.

EXHIBIT 7-2

Integration: When Tasks are Performed

When is this done

	Before Closing	Immediately After Closing	Within 90 Days	Within One Year	N/A	Response Total
1. Offer retention bonuses to selected employees	44% (34)	18% (14)	9% (7)	4% (3)	26% (20)	78
2. Revise sales commission plans	19% (14)	27% (20)	17% (13)	25% (19)	12% (9)	75
3. Obtain non-competition agreements from selected employees	44% (32)	22% (16)	4% (3)	3% (2)	27% (20)	73
4. Change company name	3% (2)	34% (23)	7% (5)	28% (19)	28% (19)	68
5. Send publicity releases	8% (6)	65% (48)	11% (8)	1% (1)	15% (11)	74
6. Replace signage on buildings and trucks	0% (0)	35% (24)	26% (18)	21% (14)	18% (12)	68
7. Send announcement to customers	8% (6)	82% (64)	8% (6)	1% (1)	1% (1)	78
8. Meet with buyers at key customers	11% (8)	45% (33)	36% (26)	4% (3)	4% (3)	73
9. Meet with key customer executives	15% (11)	36% (26)	37% (27)	7% (5)	5% (4)	73
10. Meet with sales staff one-to-one	45% (35)	45% (35)	9% (7)	1% (1)	0% (0)	78
11. Change fringe benefit programs	7% (5)	33% (23)	14% (10)	36% (25)	9% (6)	69
12. Meet with sales reps from key suppliers	27% (20)	16% (12)	39% (29)	8% (6)	11% (8)	75
13. Meet with key supplier executives	34% (25)	12% (9)	21% (15)	19% (14)	14% (10)	73
14. Issue new employee handbook; policy & procedures manual	7% (5)	40% (30)	29% (22)	16% (12)	8% (6)	75
15. Replace CEO	5% (3)	26% (15)	5% (3)	14% (8)	49% (28)	57
16. Replace CFO	4% (2)	30% (17)	14% (8)	11% (6)	41% (23)	56
17. Integrate back office functions	4% (3)	32% (24)	28% (21)	31% (23)	4% (3)	74
18. Integrate warehouse locations	4% (3)	13% (9)	34% (24)	33% (23)	16% (11)	70
19. Meet with employees in small groups	25% (18)	55% (40)	15% (11)	1% (1)	4% (3)	73
20. Hold company-wide employee meeting	10% (7)	68% (49)	14% (10)	3% (2)	6% (4)	72
21. Meet with employees one-to-one	18% (13)	31% (22)	40% (29)	6% (4)	6% (4)	72
				Total Respondents		97

Culture

Culture is like the weather, in that everybody talks about it but not enough of us do anything about it. Maybe we simply don't know what to do.

Dennis Kozlowski has been criticized for some of the things he did, but most people would agree that Tyco during his reign was masterful at integrating its many acquisitions. In *Lessons from Master Acquirers: A CEO Roundtable for Making Mergers Succeed* (Harvard Business School Press, 2000) Kozlowski recommended that acquirers "create change from the culture itself—then the company owns those changes."

Of course it's hard to integrate cultures in hostile takeovers. I don't believe in hostile takeovers; in fact, I believe a distributor would be crazy to try to make a hostile takeover. It's hard enough to integrate cultures in *friendly* acquisitions.

Here is an example. One company has a self-disciplined team accustomed to lots of freedom and responsibility within a tight framework, where the leader manages the system, not the people. (Sounds good!) Imagine integrating that group into a tightly disciplined, tyrannical organization where the leader manages the people, not the system. This combination would be as chaotic as those Sunday morning political shows on TV.

If you find an otherwise attractive acquisition, except for a bad cultural fit, my advice would be to run off in the other direction. Remember: If a distributor's value lies in its customer relationships, you have to persuade the people you've acquired (the key people who maintain those relationships) to work toward their new company's goals. In my soul, I do not believe you can lead people whose culture is incompatible with yours. Of course, you could always try to change your culture to fit that of the acquired company, but even with much persistent effort it probably wouldn't work out very well.

True story

A very large electrical distributor grew over many years by making acquisitions in nearby markets to add geographical coverage. The names of the acquired companies were changed, but those companies continued to be run as if they were local businesses.

The acquired companies were made to feel like new members of the family. Each new company was featured in the company newsletter. A human resources person was on site at the time of the closing. Overlap was avoided so that branches did not have to be closed. The only staff reductions after closing were redundant support staff. The sellers were asked to deal with non-performing people prior to the sale.

Most former owners did not stay on after a transition period. Notable exceptions were made for some who became members of the senior management.

Advice to buyers: Pick acquisition targets with the same or similar values to the buyer, for example, the way employees are valued and treated and the way customers are served. Emphasize the people side of the integration equation, in addition to finance and information systems. Culture clash must be avoided.

My friend Bruce Merrifield, consultant *nonpareil* in the distribution world, tells about the "culture binder" he created at his old company in Saint Louis. Bruce filled a three-ring binder with memos and "culture-grams" that went out to the staff at his company. Typical topics were personnel systems, sales management practices (totally new in the '70s), small-order management, and service excellence. This scrapbook of documents was written evidence of the company's culture, the way the firm did business, the way the leadership communicated to the employees, the company's values and traditions. Bruce was able to present the culture binder to his successor in an effort to help the new executive preserve that culture.

Business plan

I love business plans because they communicate expectations to the troops and provide a map of how the leader intends to reach his objective. I hate business plans because they are nearly always wrong, especially the ones that stretch too far into the future.

The wise acquisitive distributor works with the potential seller's management (at least with the owner-manager and probably the CFO) to create a multi-year business plan. The plan is designed to demonstrate that the acquisition will provide an acceptable return on investment and adequate cash flow to repay lenders and grow the business. The business plan will illustrate that the acquisition fits in with the buyer's overall strategy and put a dollar amount on the synergies of the combined businesses.

No matter how you feel about business plans, they are an important piece of the strategy phase of the acquisition process. I believe that the business plan is important to the integration phase. The plan you relied on in structuring the deal, and which was co-authored by your manager responsible for the integration, is a tool to be used to communicate with the leadership of the acquired company. There should be no doubt concerning what you are asking them to accomplish and what resources you're providing for them to do it. It's all in the business plan.

Who stays, who goes

This is the "tough love" part of the integration phase. There may be some people at the acquired company who have to go. These employees are the chronic underperformers, the deadwood, who should not be there under any circumstances. One of the best things you can do is ask the seller to let those people go before the closing. His company will be better off, even if the deal doesn't close for some reason.

People worry that the sale will result in a "Black Monday" staff reduction. Everyone knows that most acquisition plans include integration of back-office functions, elimination of redundancies and inefficiencies, etc. If that is going to happen, the integration plan needs to include how the combined companies will be organized under the new ownership. The smart thing to do (assuming an asset purchase) is to avoid hiring the people you will not be keeping on. If you need their services during a transition period, engage them as non-employees under temporary contracts. Someone will have to determine if the downside (bad feelings) outweighs the benefits. I strongly believe this arrangement is preferable, and more honorable, than keeping people around under false pretenses. They should be able to get on with their lives.

True story

A large foodservice distributor negotiated to buy a small, local distributor. Through due diligence, bankers, and suppliers, the buyer knew the target company was in some financial trouble. Discussions with the seller's key staff revealed that three of the seven people would not accept the buyer's plans for the business. The buyer decided to walk away rather than pay a large premium for what appeared to be trouble.

The target company failed shortly thereafter. The buyer purchased much of the inventory and hired the staff. The three problem people did indeed turn out to be unwilling to adapt to the buyer's strategy. The happy ending is that the remaining staff has been highly successful, and one formerly small area of the target business has become a home run.

Advice to buyers: Be prepared to walk away if serious people problems are found during due diligence. Don't hire people whom you know won't fit in. Don't take the seller's word for it: Interview the key employees yourself before closing the deal.

Special issues with distributors

Selective/exclusive supplier relationships

Supplier relationships are so important to distributors that it is not an overstatement to say that suppliers may be as important as customers. (Heresy!) Depending on the industry, supplier concentration can approach 100% of a distributor's total purchase volume. Even when the biggest supplier's product lines are only 10% of purchases, the operating profits from that vendor may be 20% or more of the total. Suffice it to say, written approval of the ownership change from key suppliers before closing may be a contingency in the deal. At a minimum, the new owner may need assurance of a vendor's continued support.

A legal opinion may be needed to understand if a particular supplier has the right to drop the distributor due to a change of ownership. Some supplier-distributor relationships are governed by formal contracts; others are not. But business success is unlikely if the supplier feels forced to continue selling to the new owner. A distributor needs the unqualified support of his most important suppliers.

Why would a supplier, especially a large one, being unwilling to support the new owner? The short answer is that distribution patterns have shifted dramatically in recent years due to mergers and acquisitions at all three levels: suppliers, distributors, and customers. Some suppliers are unhappy with some of the distributors they have and take advantage of opportunities to rationalize or reduce the number of distributors in some markets. Others have formed stronger alliances with national distributors and seek to limit the number of independent distributors where conflicts exist. In one case I consulted on, a very small printing paper distributor enjoyed a strong franchise with a major paper mill, a relationship that dated back over 75 years. The small distributor had to find the right buyer for his company, as his intrinsic value was locked up in a franchise that could not be transferred to most buyers.

An obvious problem exists when the new owner is closely aligned with a direct competitor of one of the target company's key suppliers. That type of analysis is part of the strategic phase of acquisition planning.

Unfortunately, and partly due to M&A, there aren't many valuable exclusive franchises left in the distribution world. One of the risks distributors face is the awarding of one of their important lines to a direct competitor. The careful acquisitive distributor should talk to the major vendors prior to the closing. He should try to obtain assurances of continued support, including a representation that the supplier would not add more distributors in response to the acquisition.

Meeting with suppliers during the due diligence phase is also the beginning of the supplier integration phase. The supplier investigation is yet another reason why the cloak of secrecy usually must be lifted after the financial stage of due diligence.

Closing of branch locations

Consolidation of overlapping locations is a strategy issue. The need to coordinate leases, add storage space, etc., can be time consuming. It's a good idea for the integration manager to get to work on this long before the closing.

Changing of employment practices

There shouldn't be a problem with personnel policies if there is a good cultural fit. There could be major problems, even over small issues, if the cultures don't match up well. My advice is, don't sweat the small stuff. It's not a big deal if the people at the acquired company have a few benefits that are different from those in the rest of the organization. Is it really important that each location operate in exactly the same way?

Changing sales policies

Sales policies are the guidelines management gives to the organization on how to deal with customers. Since management cannot personally deal with every customer and make every decision, the sales policies give employees the authority and responsibility to make judgments affecting customers.

During the first 100 days or so, the manager responsible for the integration process needs to take his time to understand what the company does for its customers and why. There is no need to rush these decisions. What works in one branch location may not be right for the others. Anything affecting customers needs to be changed with great care. If in doubt, leave it alone. When you're sure what needs to be done, do it.

Customer relationships with the former owner and outside sales reps

I think distributors should always have a contingency plan for the possibility that a key customer relationship person is suddenly gone from the scene. Aside from retirements and firings, just about every other departure comes as a shock.

True story

An Illinois-based specialty building materials distributor made two successful acquisitions, including a nine-location business larger than his original company.

The seller did not want the buyer to meet his general managers before closing, in case the deal fell through. The buyer felt that meeting the people was very important, especially because the former owner would be gone. Due diligence showed that the general managers were of critical importance to the business. The buyer wanted the team to understand his philosophy and direction so they could get off to a running start.

The buyer spent the first nine consecutive days after the closing (one at each of the locations) in group and individual meetings with his 300 new employees. Only one did not agree with his philosophy and chose to leave. Communication was important to the buyer, whose original company had 75 employees: He knew each person and his family personally.

His business is eight times its original size after only five years. He knew the companies he acquired: Each was a peer organization in a different geographic area.

Advice to buyers: Communicate!

Distributors with adequate backup staff have options; others don't. I am amazed by stories about the ways distributors handle sudden departures of their salespeople. The responses range from a reassuring phone call to a customer, a visit by a harried executive (sometimes followed by weeks of silence), to no contact by anyone. The customer really wants to know that he is appreciated, that his business is important, and that there is a capable problem-solver assigned to take care of him.

If the sales rep goes to a direct competitor and has not signed a non-competition agreement with the company, you have another kind of problem. A distributor in California (a state that does not enforce non-competition agreements) is said to have an interesting approach. Salespeople are organized in teams of six to eight, with a sales leader. If someone leaves, the team leader assigns all of the departed person's accounts to other members of his team. They start visiting the biggest and best accounts that same day, leaving no stones unturned. The departed person, no matter how good or hard-working he is, will have a tough time dislodging customers who are so well taken care of.

Sales commission plans

No topic gets distributors as excited as a discussion about sales compensation. It's easy to fill a room at a distributor meeting if the speaker claims to have a revolutionary new plan.

Not every division in the company must have the same commission plan for salespeople. (I do think that all salespeople doing the same work in the same location do have to be on the same plan, but that is a subject for another book.)

To most salesforces, the compensation plan is a sacred cow. I believe that management is at fault whenever I see a compensation plan that has been changed frequently. That's a sign of indecision. The sunspot cycle is 11 years. The sales compensation plan shouldn't be changed more often than that.

If, after studying the situation carefully, you feel there are good reasons to make a dramatic change, you may have to do it. But I would not make this change during the integration period. If the sales compensation situation is that bad, perhaps this company is not a good strategic fit.

Minor adjustments don't pose much of a problem. I'm not saying that periodic, even annual, changes are a problem. But don't make the patient undergo open-heart surgery too often, especially during integration.

Changing information systems

Some distributors are literally defined by their management information systems. All of their policies and procedures revolve around the system. The inputs and outputs of the business are controlled by the system.

Putting in a new system is in the same degree of difficulty as an organ transplant. The process is expensive, traumatic, takes a very long time, the results are unpredictable, and the outcome can be a total disaster. System modifications, data conversion, and user training offer many opportunities for fatal errors.

I prefer to see a fairly simple system that is dependable, thoroughly mastered by the users, and easy to maintain. Of course older, less powerful systems don't have all the features needed for electronic commerce and exotic analysis tools. Those shortcomings can often be worked around with personal computers. Regrettably, some distributors have invested much capital in exotic, state-of-the-art systems that their people don't know how to use. They may not get much more use out those systems than they did from their outdated predecessors.

A target company already using a system the buyer is familiar with, or the one the buyer uses, is a big bonus. (It might be interesting to make up a list of users of your system when looking for targets.) Changing systems shortly before or after an acquisition is a recipe for trouble.

Communication with customers, employees, and suppliers

There are too many customers and suppliers to allow for personal visits with each one. Customer profitability analysis will identify the customers (and suppliers) you most need to communicate with. Ideally, discussions during the due diligence process will help identify customers and suppliers with whom there is likely to be a transition problem.

Meetings with employees individually and in groups

A group forum does not provide an ideal opportunity for two-way communication. The best chance to find out what concerns an employee is a private conversation. To the extent possible, one-to-one conversations with key employees during the due diligence process will enable you to get your message across and identify employees who aren't likely to support your plans for the business. Rumors are inevitable. The best way to minimize damage is to preempt them with good communications.

Changing company identity

Having the right to change the target company's name does not mean that the change will be beneficial. Some distributors eliminate all traces of the former owner; others choose to use the existing name indefinitely. A transitional approach might be to introduce the new owner along with the existing name, perhaps over a period of years ("An XYZ company," "Part of the XYZ Group," "Division XYZ Company").

I am reminded of a large tire retailer in Northern Ohio, formerly known as Mueller Tire. The Mueller name was synonymous with customer care and integrity in an industry that was sometimes held in low regard by consumers. Mueller won many awards for its customer programs. Yet the new owner was quick to tear down the Mueller signs and change the respected identity.

The suppliers and employees know who the ultimate owner is. The important question is, what makes sense to the customers and will result in the most business? If you bought a company with such a bad reputation that you could not wait to change its name, I would wonder why you bought it in the first place. Such an acquisition might fall under the category of turnarounds, beyond the scope of this book.

New CEO & CFO

If you are going to make a change at the top, possibly including the chief financial officer, it should not come as a surprise. Make the arrangements before the closing and implement the change quickly. It's a bad idea to make reassuring, supportive statements about the top people and then let them go a short time later. Employees don't like to be misled. They don't trust those who betray people to whom they have been loyal. If the former leaders were not doing a good enough job, the employees already know it. They may be relieved if the replacements are an obvious improvement.

Financial executives know their technical skills are readily transferable and that the financial leaders are often the first to be replaced in an acquisition. Some acquirers feel the need to install their own people in critical financial oversight functions. Unfortunately, this practice sometimes results in the loss of strong contributors with critical knowledge of the business.

Anticipating demands of high-production salespeople

Sports fans have been amazed by the salaries owners pay their star players and what they will pay to lure stars away from other teams ever since the Yankees paid Boston $100,000-plus for Babe Ruth in 1920.

Distribution executives have been known to pay princely sums to recruit star salespeople from other companies. There is a school of thought that stealing top salespeople from the competition is the poor man's way to make an acquisition. Why pay for the whole company when you can get its best customers at a discount? If the going commission rate in a particular line of trade or market is 25% to 30% of gross profit, a competitor may offer 50% or even 60% commission. A minimum compensation amount may be guaranteed for six months, a year, or longer. The buyer knows that he can't afford to pay commissions at such a high rate indefinitely, but he grabs the chance to add some large new customers and hopes the added volume will help cover his costs. This is short-term thinking, but sometimes the customers stay after the sales rep is long gone.

The competition for talented people can heat up when companies change hands. Competing distributors know that ownership changes can be stressful and that worried salespeople may be vulnerable to an approach from a neighbor offering an attractive package. I recall one situation where a sales rep hired an attorney to solicit bids for his services. The market for talent can drive up the compensation needed to hold on to top salespeople.

CHAPTER EIGHT

Special issues with owner-managed businesses

"Treat the company well. It was not a gift from your parents. It is a loan from your children."

Adapted from an old Kenyan proverb
• •

Prospective sellers may become fixated on a price they feel they must obtain for the business. The following personal story is about a group of entrepreneurs and how they valued their companies.

Walt Sutton, a speaker at my TEC group (an education organization for CEOs) meeting in 1998 told the attendees he was interested in buying their companies. He asked each of them to write down a price on a piece of paper, fold it, and pass it to the front of the room. It took no more than three minutes for the speaker to start writing the prices on an easel pad, ranging from $2 million to $100 million. Most of the prices were in the $5 million to $10 million range. Did the price have to do with the operating earnings of the businesses or the net book values? No, the prices were based on the perceptions of how much money each person felt he would need to live the rest of his life in worry-free luxury! The ensuing group discussion revealed their thinking about how much (pretax) proceeds they would need to cover security for themselves and their families, to provide the lifestyle they were used to, and to indulge in one or two of their fantasies. The rest of the discussion was about golf, travel, and boats.

This is not to say that people will arbitrarily put a price tag on a fabulous company based on their personal needs. But the personal-needs minimum will set a floor under which the owner does not wish to part with his business. Barring unusual circumstances, such as a troubled business or a health crisis, why would a generally optimistic business owner trade his perceived financial security for something less?

The CEO's family members

The owner-manager is sometimes but not always the controlling shareholder of the family distribution business. An older, multigenerational business may have a highly complex ownership with the vestiges of preceding generations: uncles, aunts, cousins, trusts and trustees, bank trust officers, non-profit organizations, distant relatives of deceased key employees from many years ago, etc. Some of the passive owners (passive because they aren't actively employed by the business) may truly be passive owners, rarely if ever calling the CEO and uninterested even in seeing annual financial statements. Other passive owners are anything but: They call the CEO often, demand to be represented on the board, pore over monthly financial reports, and question decisions, especially those affecting their dividend or rent payments. In nastier situations, unhappy passive shareholders hire attorneys to assist them.

The CEO in this situation has a tough enough job running the company on a day-to-day basis. He would have a very tough time gaining everyone's support for a sale of the company's assets. He fears litigation and simply may not have the energy to open a can of worms. It may take a patient and creative acquirer to assist the CEO (who indeed wants to sell) in unlocking the value hidden in his company. There are still lots of these companies around, and they have not changed hands—even though everyone would truly be better off if they did—for the reasons stated above.

The majority owner will sometimes pave the way for a trans-action by buying out the minority owners prior to selling the company. This is helpful to the buyer. The existence of look-back agreements may affect the owner-manager's willingness to sell the business. Look-back agreements are sometimes used in stock redemptions to protect minority sellers. The buyer agrees to share some of the proceeds from the sale of the company within a certain period of time following the redemption. These agreements often feature a sliding scale with gradually reduced sharing of the sales proceeds over a period of one to three years.

Estate planning and income taxes

It is a blessing for the buyer if the target company has an experienced, sophisticated outside accountant. I was involved in a deal where the prospective seller's accountant advised her not to sell because he did not understand changes made in the tax code over six years ago.

Sometimes it is helpful to arrange a meeting between your advisors and the seller's advisors. They can work out misunderstandings about the income tax and estate tax implications of a proposed transaction.

Many owner-managed distributors have been set up as pass-through entities for income tax reasons and are owned by family limited partnerships for gift and estate tax planning purposes. These entities are not impediments to business transactions, but the seller (and buyer) need qualified tax advisors to optimize the tax advantages for everyone.

Lifestyle businesses

Some owner-managers maintain little or no boundary between their business and personal lives. The business checkbook pays for some expenses (health care, life insurance, cars, dining, sports tickets, clubs, condos, travel) that are at least partly personal in nature. The owner-manager may simply give himself a salary increase or a bonus whenever he needs some money. The retirement plan at the business may be the owner-manager's principal investment outside the business. The owner-manager may lease real estate to the business and have loans between him and the company. All of this financial mish-mash is complicated when the business is set up as a pass-through entity that pays its income taxes by distributing cash to the owner, who reports the company's taxable income on his personal income tax return.

There are two issues of deal-making significance for the lifestyle business. First, the owner depends on the business for all of his financial needs. He will assess the financial aspects of selling the company differently than an owner who has significant wealth outside the company. Second, there will be an elaborate series of add-backs to understand the earning potential of the business under new ownership. In these circumstances, the owner-manager will be eager to be sure that the list of add-backs is complete in order to maximize your earnings projections and his selling price.

Non-family employees

The owner-manager may have key non-family employees whom he wants to reward for their loyal service. He may also want to gain their support for the proposed transaction (or at least to minimize their fear and resistance). This is an interest you share with the owner-manager. Both of you are eager to retain the services of those employees who are crucial to the success of the company under your ownership.

The owner-manager may share some of the sales proceeds with his key people, or possibly cut them into any earn-out you negotiate. This incentive may be beneficial to you as the new owner, but of course the employees recognize where the money is coming from.

This discussion also suggests that the key employees are made aware of the transaction before the closing, possibly long before.

Advisory boards and other advisors

The owner-manager's circle of advisors may be wider than you think. Many distributors have formed advisory boards of experienced executives, many who know quite a bit about mergers and acquisitions. You may never meet these people, but you can be certain they will meet to analyze your proposal and to advise the owner-manager on negotiating strategy and tactics. I'm a strong advocate of advisory boards for owner-managed businesses. I have helped companies establish advisory boards and personally have served on many over the last 20 years. The advice the seller receives will only be helpful in keeping the transaction on track and serving the seller's best interests.

Many owner-managers belong to CEO education and assistance organizations like YPO and TEC. The CEOs attend monthly meetings of 12 to 15 other owner-managers who share information and give each other advice about transactions such as selling the company. Your proposed transaction will be discussed there, if your prospective seller belongs to such a group.

The traditional business advisors for most owner-managers are the accountant and the attorney. You will probably meet several times with both. The more experienced and sophisticated they are, the better for everyone. A possible downside is scheduling their time. The deal may be held up if the seller's advisors (or yours) are very busy with transactions for other clients. It's helpful for someone to prepare a complete list of contact information for all parties involved in the transaction, including e-mail, fax, home phone, home fax, cell phone numbers, and executive assistant contact information.

Family-owned real estate

Real-estate assets are a two-edged sword. The real estate is a potential source of contention if both parties want the facility, or if neither party wants the facility. The seller has a problem if he owns a run-down facility in the wrong part of town; the problem is even worse if the property faces environmental challenges. He may want to sell the property as part of the deal or lease it to the buyer to generate some income. You as the buyer may want no part of it, especially if you plan to consolidate the acquired company into one of your own facilities. If the seller has an excellent property, he may want to continue owning it as an investment. This would not present a problem if the buyer were agreeable to leasing the building or relocating. My experience is that most acquisitive distributors do not want to tie their capital up in real estate. The lease terms will be part of the negotiations for the transaction, and the lease document will be signed as part of the closing.

Life insurance policies on family members

Life insurance policies owned by the seller's business are typically not included in the transaction. The owner may continue to pay the premiums himself, cash them in, or use them in his planning for his family's financial security.

Desire to play continuing role in business

On the subject of staying on at the company after it is sold, owner-managers are roughly divided into two groups: those who want to get out of the business as soon as possible and those who would like to keep working there as though they still own it.

Those who want to get out as soon as possible will agree to stay on long enough to assure a smooth transition. They rightly see this as something they have to do to reassure the buyer. In many cases they don't intend to stick around very long, or to work very hard. The buyer may quickly tire of seeing the former owner arriving late, leaving early, and spending most of his time engaged in small talk with his former employees. The buyer may be content to know the former owner is available for consultation if needed, but there will probably be few reasons to call upon his services.

Owners who want to continue working after the change in ownership may want to negotiate a two-, three-, or five-year employment contract as part of the sale. It is important to have a meeting of the minds about the seller's expectations. The buyer may see the compensation package as part of the purchase price. This arrangement can be attractive to the buyer. The payments are deferred and the compensation is deductible for income tax purposes (although there are some additional costs such as payroll taxes and other fringe benefits). The buyer may be reluctant to tell the owner-manager that his services aren't really needed or wanted beyond the transition period. In extreme cases, the former owner-manager may see himself playing a key role in the buyer's organization. There could be bitter disappointment later if that is not what the buyer had in mind.

I know a former owner-manager who has stayed on with the new owner for many years. This individual had owned and operated his family's old and prosperous but fairly small manufacturing business. He is a masterful salesperson, and he has a small group of very important and loyal customers whom he handles personally. The new owner is a younger man, a financial buyer, who owns some other businesses. The former owner, now nearing age 80, continues to work part time handling some of the company's largest accounts. The new owner has never worked in the business on a full-time basis.

The new owner's lack of daily involvement is undoubtedly one of the keys to this unusual success story.

Most of my other stories of former owner-managers who wanted to continue working don't have a happy ending. Many of the independent distributors who sold their companies to industry consolidators with expectations of playing a major role in the company found themselves unemployed and bitter after a year or two. At least they had money in their pockets. The aftermath of some of the distribution rollups is worse, as the former owner-managers were both unemployed and poor. My advice to buyers is to be as honest as possible with the owner-managers of their acquisition targets. An effort to be kind by holding back on the truth or to avoid scaring the owner-manager away from the deal may backfire. Some of those bad feelings can have a ripple effect with the company's long-time employees.

Desire for security for employees

Being an owner-manager is sometimes a lonely job. The people at work, especially the inner circle, are often the people with whom the CEO spends most of his time, even more than with his own family. The time together in the office, over lunches, business dinners, and business trips can create strong feelings of loyalty.

The owner-manager knows who in his "kitchen cabinet" is critical to the company's success. He may try to secure employment contracts for them with the new buyer. Depending on the situation and the talents of the individuals, employment contracts may be very much in the buyer's interests.

I am a big advocate of non-competition agreements (in those places where they are legally enforceable) for key employees in distribution. Due to the intense competition for quality people and the low barriers of entry, these agreements can be the cornerstone of value for a distributor. If the buyer favors employment agreements for key people, knowing that such agreements are mostly for the protection of the employees and not the company, obtaining an enforceable non-competition agreement is likely to be of great value.

Getting into the owner's mind

Let's take a moment to look at the world through the eyes of the distributor owner-manager. The owner-manager may fit into one or more of the following categories:

- The CEO who is also majority owner is chief executive officer but, more aptly, *chief executive owner*. Like a Supreme Court justice, a federal judge (or dictator of a third-world country), he has his job for life. He may be the founder of the business, or perhaps he purchased the business and built it up, or he may be a descendant of the founder.

- The *third generation owner-CEO*, a baby boomer who owns and runs a business founded by his grandparents before World War II and built up by his parents after World War II. He was born between 1946 and 1956. He was lucky enough to get a good education and, hopefully, had the chance to work somewhere else before he started his way up the ladder (also hopefully) at the family's distribution business. He may have joined the business temporarily, but he has been there ever since.

- The *frequent-flyer owner-manager* is a person on the go. He has little support staff, so he feels the need to be everywhere at once, running from meeting to meeting, from customer to supplier, from the office to the airport.

The lives of these owner-managers, and other types and permutations, have much in common. There is little or no boundary between their business and personal lives. They work on personal matters at the office during the day and deal with business problems at night or on the weekends at home.

They may have financial pressures. They may be wealthy on paper, but typically most of their wealth is invested in the business. Whatever debts the business has may be their debts also, sometimes because of personal guarantees. Even if the owner does not sign on the company's debt, his stock will be worthless if the debts aren't paid. Owners are keenly aware of their dependence on the cash flow of the business and the cash needs of the company.

Owner-managers almost certainly have time pressures. With little to no support staff, the owner's time is stretched very thin. There are demands on his time from customers, suppliers, employees, lenders, and other business contacts. The owner-manager is often part of community activities (the board of the hospital, the college, the church, United Way). The owner-manager may be a member of a CEO support group such as YPO or TEC, or he may serve on the board of directors of one or two other companies. All of these business obligations are added to the demands of his family.

Owner-managers can be somewhat isolated, in spite of the fact that they are seldom alone. Many of their business relationships are superficial. The relationships that have depth are with inner-circle employees, who, as employees, may be reluctant to be totally open with their boss.

Besides himself and his spouse, the owner-manager may have business obligations to the generation before him (his parents) and the generation after (his children). The preceding generation may still rely on the business for their income and financial security; the next generation may be depending on the business for future employment and financial security.

It's lonely at the top. Many owner-managers establish an advisory board to act as a sounding board, provide unbiased advice, and to help relieve the constant pressure. The advisory board usually plays an important role in the prospective sale of an owner-managed business. Advisory board members are usually experienced executives, one or more of whom may have an extensive background with transactions. The advisory board will provide guidance as well as ensure that the owner-manager gets quality professional advice. The advisory board plays the important role of helping the owner-manager stay calm during the sale process. Some owner-managers get the same sort of help from their YPO or TEC group in a more limited fashion.

The acquirer may have little or no contact with the advisory board, but it is important to know who they are and to understand their role.

CHAPTER NINE

What Sellers Should Expect

"Let us be thankful for the fools. But for them the rest of us could not succeed."

Mark Twain
• • • • • • •

Some acquirers buy companies all the time. They have experienced people, an established process they use to handle transactions, and a seasoned group of advisors to assist them with the details. The buyer's acquisition team may be working on numerous deals, in various stages, at the same time. The chances of the buyer's acquisition staff getting emotionally involved in a transaction are pretty low.

Most prospective sellers are engaged in a once-in-a-lifetime event. They have been involved in the sale of a large business before and will probably not do so again. The seller does not have an experienced staff, a process to follow or a team of advisors whom he knows well from prior deals. The prospective seller has no other deals in the works, and may not be in touch with any other prospective buyers for his company. The chance of the prospective seller's getting emotionally involved in the transaction is 100%.

The prospective seller may be a lone wolf. The seller may not be able or willing to confide in any of his key staff due to fear of word about the deal leaking out. Even the seller's financial officer may be left out of the early discussions.

The buyer's vantage point

The prospective seller needs to understand the basics of the acquisition process from the buyer's viewpoint. To start with, the seller must recognize different types of buyers and their varying objectives.

Different types of buyers

Who are the buyers? They can be categorized as follows:

- Investment groups: It's just another investment in their portfolio.

- Manufacturers and retailers: don't understand the dynamics of distribution; buying an outlet for their products (manufacturers) or a low-cost supplier (retailers).

- Distributors from other lines of trade: may not recognize the differences from one type of distributor to another.

- Individuals: including cashed-out entrepreneurs and retired executives from big companies; both feel they are business experts who can run anything.

- Rollups and other industry consolidators: Could be an investment firm or another distributor; they almost always know a great deal more about finance than about running a customer-focused business.

- Competing distributors: have the distinct advantage of understanding your business and being able to see both the existing value and the potential.

Types of mistakes typical of each type of buyer

Most of these buyer types don't understand distribution and some don't even know what to look for.

The distribution business is based more on intangibles than most other businesses. The value of customer relationships and the importance of key salespeople are not well understood. Much of the value of distributors is simply invisible, especially when compared to retail stores, manufacturing equipment, etc. The nature of business-to-business customer relationships is harder to understand and quantify than business-to-consumer or manufacturer-distributor relationships.

A distributor is a special kind of vendor. The barriers of entry and exit are low and it is very easy for customers to change suppliers. If the acquirer does not understand the added value of distributors, especially the fragile nature of relationships, the customer who has many alternatives can easily go elsewhere.

The distributor is also wedded to his information systems platform. Large acquirers, especially those with highly developed MIS expertise, expect to integrate their acquisitions onto a powerful, company-wide enterprise system. In some cases they never got around to it, leaving the smaller companies on their own systems due to the cost and disruption of making changes. Some distributors concentrate their acquisition searches on targets already using the same software package as the acquiring company. Other acquirers avoid targets with antiquated systems, or those who have switched to a new system within the most recent year or two.

Staying in the game

There are two types of distributors: the buyers and the bought. If you want to continue to occupy a seat at the giant poker table of distributor owners, don't sell your business. Working for someone else is not the same as playing with your own chips. Playing your own hand is not the same as having someone watching over your shoulder, or reaching into your cards. And watching someone else play isn't really that much fun, once you have done it all yourself.

Your people

No one else will treat your people exactly the way you do. They won't think so and neither will you. Things will be different—better in some ways and not as good in others. Be honest with them—the way you would hope to be treated if the shoe were on the other foot.

An ownership change can be a very good thing for many of the people who used to work for you. The most talented, adaptable workers may find opportunities with the new organization that you could never have given them. A capable buyer with strong financing and a commitment to invest in the business may be the best thing that ever happened to some of the employees. Many may find the change of ownership to be a non-event, seeing little difference in their daily work lives after the acquisition.

Acquisitions can mean nothing but heartache for the employees of the acquired company, depending on the industry. This is generally not true in distribution. The enlightened buyer realizes the importance of the people to the customer relationships he is paying for. Some employees, such as sales and support people who are the keepers of those important relationships, are the very reason the buyer wants the company. There is a shortage of skilled workers at all levels in distribution. Finally, distribution companies are unlike factories that can be moved to another state. Some specific non-customer contact jobs may be eliminated or relocated, especially when the buyer has a facility in the same market.

Your birthright

Esau sold his birthright to Jacob, his twin, for a bowl of soup. If you consider your business to be your birthright, and you are thinking about selling it, consider the price you are willing to accept.

If your family name is on the front door, and that is important to you, you are selling the right to change that name. If you want to the business to keep that name, don't sell it unless the price is worth the unhappiness. The name will be changed. Thomas Edison never forgave J.P. Morgan for changing the name of Edison's company to General Electric.

If your great-grandfather started the business, and your grandfather and your father ran it before you did, you are selling the right to have your son or daughter succeed you. If you want your family to continue to run the business, don't sell it unless the price is worth it. Your child will not be asked to run this company.

Selling your soul to the devil

Owner-managers are in some ways a tormented bunch. Many owners of multi-generational businesses start feeling their obligations to the next generation almost as soon as they complete paying their debts to the one that preceded them. Those owner-managers are trying to beat the third-generation jinx that predicts failure for most businesses under third-generation ownership.

Many owner-managers find themselves faced with a dilemma: What's better for the next generation—selling the business now, or keeping it with the hope that at least one member of the family will want to take it over some day? This question is called when a qualified buyer appears with a reasonably attractive offer.

Experienced buyers long for the opportunity to take a close look at the financial details of an attractive business. By placing a strong offer on the table, buyers know that the prospective seller and his advisors will engage in a sacred ritual: How much would be left after paying off liabilities, minority shareholders, taxes and deal expenses? What annual income could be expected from the proceeds? Will there be enough to maintain a certain lifestyle, to provide for the family, to make gifts to charity?

If the numbers look good, the prospective seller may start to fantasize about what life would be like, and about the advantages of being able to travel, play golf and go boating.

Once a prospective seller starts spending that money in his mind, his negotiating position may weaken dramatically. This is called selling your soul to the devil. Don't do it.

Lessons from *The Prince*: expectations vs. reality

Poor Niccolo Machiavelli wasn't really such a bad guy; he is just misunderstood. Machiavelli was a long-time civil servant who took the trouble to write down his observations about what worked, and what didn't work, in the politics of Italy in the 16th century. He was not the person in charge, but in his role close to the boss he was able to learn the rules of the game. Some of the rules that Machiavelli authored pertain to the business of acquiring a company. One of those rules was this:

> When taking over a principality you only have to do two things: Kill the previous prince and his whole family and do not change the current laws and taxes.

Most successful acquirers may not be able to quote from *The Prince,* but many of Machiavelli's rules are second nature to them. Sellers, take note.

Poor George Westinghouse. He ran his companies for progress, for his people, and for profits. Thinking the founder to be a poor manager, the moneymen finally gained control of Westinghouse Electric and ran it strictly for profit. Westinghouse lived until 1914 but never got over the changes made after he was pushed out.

If you sell your company with the expectation that you will continue to work there for a long time, in a role similar to the one you are accustomed to, you are not being realistic. No matter what was said during the negotiations, you are being unrealistic. You may beat the odds, but the chances of this happening are about the same as winning the lottery. If you're feeling that lucky, maybe you should buy a lottery ticket.

Advisors

Ironically, the owner-manager may be supremely confident (overconfident) about his ability to negotiate the sale transaction without outside help. An executive who has piloted his business successfully for years—avoiding the shoals, dealing skillfully with customers, suppliers, employees, lenders, and politicians—feels supremely confident. Such a leader may not anticipate too much of a challenge when faced with financial types who don't really understand the business.

Tragically, the owner with a long history of vanquishing the competition may stumble when working on the biggest sale of his life. A distribution owner-manager in upstate New York was known for his skill in assembling his large business through shrewd acquisitions. Ironically, he was a victim of selling his company to one of the failed industry rollups described in an earlier chapter.

Stalking horse

Buyers like to work on acquisitions where the seller is not negotiating with anyone else. A primary reason is that buyers are usually able to pay a smaller premium when they aren't forced to compete with another suitor.

Just because the seller prefers not having another suitor does not automatically mean that you're better off playing one buyer off another. An auction may not be in your best interests, depending on the circumstances.

In general, I think sellers should have at least two qualified buyers lined up. Competition does tend to bring better offers.

Here are some of the possible negatives:

- The auction may scare some good buyers away. They don't want to invest the time and money on a transaction with a low likelihood of success.

- The auction process forces you to open your books to several prospective buyers, some of whom may just be fishing for information, which can be used against you in the marketplace.

- The process may make your feel forced to sell the business to someone, even if the offers are disappointing. The company may be seen as shopworn if you ultimately decide not to sell.

Confidentiality

The larger the buyer's organization, the sooner word of the deal will leak out. It's almost impossible to keep secrets in big companies due to the anonymity factor: leaks can't be traced when so many people are in on the secret. The lethal grapevine of security leaks in distribution is through the network of suppliers. Many acquirers canvass supplier personnel as part of their deal planning and, later, due diligence. The acquirers want background information about the pros and cons of buying various competing distributors. They want to know if the suppliers will support the change in ownership. Supplier employees, especially sales people, tend to confide in the salespeople and buyers at their distributors. Despite the usual pledges of confidentiality, and sincere efforts to comply, the "need to know" network in most acquirers is too large to prevent such leaks.

It's far better for the prospective seller's people to hear about what's going on from the seller himself. Most employees are sophisticated and alert enough to understand the owner's position and appreciate the respect shown to them by their leader. The owner-manager then has the opportunity to preempt the rumor mill and provide his side of the story. If the "secret" deal becomes widely known and then falls through, the prospective seller has breached the trust of his people and endangered morale.

Buyers well know the sensitivity of the confidentiality issue, and some try to use the seller's fear against him. Many buyers have renegotiated the pending deal with the owner, knowing that he worries about holding the company together should the deal fall through.

Curb appeal

Many buyers are afraid of buying a distributor who has recently undergone a change in senior management, implemented a new software system, or relocated its main operation. These traumas may destabilize a distribution business, causing it to lose key employees and customers. Some buyers would rather wait until the business is back to normal.

Think of the process of selling residential real estate. A property with recent repairs can arouse a buyer's suspicion. A house with many minor flaws can cause concerns about the underlying structure. A cluttered interior may prevent the buyer from seeing the potential of the property. A home with genuine curb appeal looks good as the buyer pulls into the driveway, has no telltale signs of patching up, is immaculate and free of clutter. All of the systems are in good working order and there are no obvious flaws, however minor (leaky faucets).

The same logic applies to distribution businesses. Companies with great curb appeal have dependable information systems with well-trained users, prompt and accurate financial reporting, and excellent housekeeping. They don't have mountains of stale inventory and they don't have ancient receivables on the credit reports. The people are professional, presentable, and friendly.

Even if your company is not for sale, the likelihood of an attractive unsolicited offer coming over the transom is a lot better on a well-run ship. A side benefit of having a company with curb appeal is that it is much easier, and a lot more fun, to run one of those than a fixer-upper.

The seller's story

Everyone loves a good story. That is how we learn and how mankind passes knowledge from one generation to the next. It's a good idea to have a well-rehearsed story about your business. For example, the people at your company should be readily able to explain important information such as what the company does, why its customers buy from the company, and what the company's values are. Taking this a step further, the company's leaders should be able to explain where the company is going, why it's going there, and how it will get there. This information is important to the people who work there and to the people who do business with the company. It is also if vital importance to prospective buyers.

Buyers like to know that the people at the company have a strong sense of purpose and a clearly defined direction. Buyers need to be able to visualize how the company would be successful under their ownership. Buyers love to have a story to relate about the proposed acquisition to their people, their directors, and their lenders.

If you have some exciting initiatives under way, weave them into your story about the company. Create a vision of the future of the enterprise with new customer segments, new products and services, and new geographic markets. The story may tie in to your reasons for selling, including the need for capital and more skilled people. It's great to have a detailed strategic plan, but it's more important to have a good story that conveys your vision and enthusiasm for the company's future.

Changing the purchase price

Don't be surprised or offended if the buyer comes back after due diligence and tries to change the purchase price as stated in the letter of intent. Even if the buyer states that he never (well, almost never) tries to "nibble," many do. They may find that recent sales are trending below expectations, that economic conditions are deteriorating, or that the buyer has become worried about globalization or whatever.

Buyers often try to revise the purchase price (downward, of course). You will have to decide the sincerity/validity of the request, evaluate the reasoning behind this, and decide what your response will be. This is often part of the game; so don't get mad unless you think that cutting off the discussions is in your best interest.

Delaying tactics

Buyers sometimes need to delay closings for legitimate reasons, and occasionally they stall them deliberately. The buyer may want to wait to see more results from the business, to await the outcome of a contract renewal or a labor negotiation. Advisors (notoriously attorneys) and lenders working on the transaction often cause delays.

Delays are common and are usually in good faith. You will have to get the facts and make a judgment as to how long of a delay you are willing to accept. There are also many risks to the buyer in delaying the closing (you may find another buyer or change your mind about selling). Don't expect everything to go smoothly or exactly according to schedule.

Good cops/bad cops and other tricks

Poker, especially Texas Hold 'Em, has been riding a wave of popularity since broadcasters starting putting high-stakes games on TV. Poker fans and other students of human nature enjoy watching the way different characters (and I do mean characters) play what is really a fairly simple game.

Like poker, there are many ways to play your hand when negotiating a business transaction. Use of negotiating tricks— including dirty tricks—depends on the person. Some people either rely on playing games or disdain them as a matter of personal preference. Buying and selling businesses is a high-stakes enterprise. Unlike a poker game, the process is very complicated and usually takes a long time.

The seller needs to be prepared for anything when negotiated the sale of his business. People still play the old good-cop, bad-cop game. Some players make outrageous demands and then make tiny concessions. Buyers try to hook the seller with a very attractive proposal and work backwards later on. Be prepared for nibblers, screamers, and people with conveniently poor memories.

Junk mail and voice messages from strangers

Hungry financial intermediaries send countless business development letters and make endless phone calls to owner managers. Owners of distribution businesses are high on the list of juicy prospects. Many owner managers have a knee-jerk reaction to most or all of these solicitations. I suspect that many envelopes are tossed into the wastebasket unopened, and most of the voice messages go unanswered. The vast majority of these inquiries are bogus and don't deserve any attention.

Unfortunately, the barrage of junk mail and calls has conditioned owner-managers to ignore all inquiries from strangers. Legitimate investment bankers and other sincere inquirers have trouble getting through. The clever ones can get through all but the most impermeable barriers unless the prospect makes it so difficult that even the most persistent efforts aren't successful.

Owner-managers who cannot be bothered to separate the wheat from the chaff may miss out on the contact that would be the deal they have been dreaming of. I am a follower of the theory that nearly everything is for sale if the price is right.

Owner managers need to be prepared for these inquiries. I propose a process:

- Toss the obvious garbage.

- Do a little homework on the inquiries that may be legitimate. Research the firm and the individual to see if they are legitimate.

- Forward the inquiries that pass scrutiny to an outsider, such as a member of your advisory board. Ask the outside advisor to phone the person and screen the inquiry by evaluating the firm, the caller, and the legitimacy of the inquiry. The identity of the buyer should be provided as well as background information.

- The outside advisor will gather whatever information he can for consideration by the owner-manager and possibly the advisory board. The company will decide if, and how, to respond to the information request from the prospective buyer.

- Many owner-managers would like to know what outsiders feel their company is worth. It will be necessary to provide some information about the business. Summary financial data can be very basic and need reveal nothing about the company's customers, employees, or suppliers. Most buyers are willing to start pricing discussions based on a brief summary of recent income statements and a current balance sheet.

- The owner-manager who is unwilling to share any information may ask the prospective buyer to describe his valuation methodology. The company can apply the valuation mechanics to its data and estimate the value.

Investment bankers will do an appraisal on a fee basis. Some firms will consider applying the fee towards a large contingent fee for helping the client find a buyer. Many investment bankers are eager to do a valuation, since this is often the first step toward sale of the business.

An appraisal for the purpose of sale is usually much less costly than a valuation for estate-planning purposes. Valuations for tax purposes include an extraordinary amount of documentation justifying the valuation and discounting methods, technical tax information, and the appraiser's qualifications. Estimates of potential selling price are less time consuming.

Some acquirers of distribution businesses may not be as smart about the industry as they think they are. They can be like colonists occupying a new land where the natives already know how to run the place.

Both large and small distributor acquisitions are likely to fail, for these reasons:

- Buyers often bite off more than they can chew, both in terms of finances and management time, skill, and commitment.

- Buyers are tempted to jump to another pond rather than go to an adjacent lily pad. A distributor in Queens may be better off acquiring a company in Brooklyn than in Albany.

- Buyers may become victims of trying to venture out too far without proper intelligence about where they are headed.

- Buyers may lack the discipline to stick to their strategy (good choice of targets); to negotiate well (good choice of weapons); to perform proper due diligence (good intelligence), and occupy well (good integration).

- Some buyers lack the sensitivity to understand the selling method used by distributors and do not recognize the value added by salespeople.

The process by which mistakes occur varies, but the effect can be the same. Buyers spend operating money on the purchase price and can't afford to invest in the business following acquisition.

Even two companies in the same line of trade in the same city may speak the same language but be unable to communicate. Depending on the circumstances, one distributor buying another is certainly more likely to be successful than other buyers. He may fail, however, if he tries to impose his own playbook before he fully understands the company he acquired.

He who is most likely to succeed is

- Another distributor
- From a nearby market
- With complementary products
- And a similar culture
- Who has customers with similar needs and relationship dynamics
- And uses a similar method of establishing and securing his customer relationships.

Acquisitive distributors, with everything else going for them, sometimes succumb to an error of geography. They fail to recognize the importance of acquiring a lily pad close enough to drive to and from in a single day.

Some managers will try very hard to avoid making an overnight business trip. If the management team is not willing to make those sacrifices, or to relocate altogether, there won't be much face-to-face contact between the buyer and seller. This may be a blessing in disguise, or a big problem.

Some buyers eventually become insecure with the hands-off management approach and start to meddle or, worse, attempt to run the remote location by telephone and e-mail. This can be much worse than regular, personal visits. Visits by top management to the remote location are much more effective and less disruptive than branch manager visits to headquarters.

The buyers with the greatest likelihood of failure are those with unrealistic expectations. Some investors entered the distribution arena in the late '90s looking for technology-style returns, such as a private-equity firm shooting for 30% compounded annual returns and an exit within five to seven years. This type of investor expects to take his profits, withdraw his capital, and move on. This type of buyer will, of course, be disappointed (or worse).

Most buyers are woefully unprepared, information-wise.

- They will skip or make short shrift of business due diligence. This may be for cost reasons or in response to time pressures. Much due diligence that could (or should) be performed by outside experts will be done by inexperienced company employees or not at all.

- "Market due diligence," different from business due diligence, pertains to study of the industry, geographic market differences, and customer demographics. It should be performed prior to identifying acquisition targets. This step is often overlooked.

- Buyers fail to do their homework in the strategy phase. They go in blind—almost aimlessly, as though in a maze— and grab the first company that looks good to them. They don't know how much to pay and lack discipline in making that determination.

- Buyers lose sight of their strategy (if they had one on the first place) during the acquisition process. The process would work more smoothly if they planned their work and worked their plan, but it usually doesn't happen that way.

Contingent purchase price and other claims

Buyers often offer a contingent purchase price when pressed by the seller for a higher price than the buyer is willing or able to pay. This condition poses some challenges.

- Can the parties agree on objective, measurable criteria to avoid future disputes over the amount due?

- Can the buyer provide adequate assurance to the seller that he will be able to make the payment out of sources other than the acquired company if necessary?

- Can the seller feel comfortable that the buyer will not try to avoid paying the contingent amount by making offsetting claims?

Regarding offsetting claims: A word of caution is needed. It is not uncommon for buyers to assert claims that the seller was overpaid due to inventory discrepancies, unrecorded liabilities, professional fees, tax claims, employment related issues, etc. Buyers have also been known to make claims, justified or otherwise, that sellers failed to comply with non-competition or non-solicitation agreements. Disputes also may arise between the buyer and seller in relation to real-estate leases between the parties.

CHAPTER TEN

Why Acquisitions Fail

"Life consists not in holding good cards but in playing those you hold well."

Josh Billings
· · · · · · ·

How many times have you heard or read that most acquisitions, no matter the industry, fail? Estimates of failure range as high as 70%. One observer claims that investors lost more shareholder value between 1995 and 2000 through failed acquisitions than they lost in the collapse of the tech stock bubble (*Angel Customers and Demon Customers*, Selden & Colvin, 2003).

These shocking statistics come from large public companies. The most well known stories are about mega-mergers in the telecommunications and financial services industries. These are some of the largest mergers ever, and it is true that the shareholders were left worse off (at least for now) by those transactions.

Some of the best and brightest business minds were behind those deals. Cynics have noted that smart investment bankers and other advisors made plenty for themselves while the investors suffered huge losses. How could smart, experienced executives have such a poor record with their most important decisions?

Look at the balance sheet, not just the P&L statement

The M&A valuation question I hear most often from distributor CEOs is, "How much are buyers paying for companies these days, in terms of multiples of earnings?" Earnings multiples are a simple formula for valuation based on multiplying the most recent year's pretax operating profits times a "magic number" to determine the selling price. The focus of attention is mostly on the income statement rather than the balance sheet or other factors.

The emphasis on earnings is natural in the current EBITDA environment, but it is a misleading indicator of company value.

The profit number by itself does not tell you anything about the company's return-on-investment potential under new ownership.

The business will have an entirely different balance sheet after a purchase. The most dramatic change is the typical transaction in which the buyer pays a premium over net book value for the assets acquired. In most cases, much of the money for the acquisition will be borrowed.

Buyers of distributors almost always purchase assets (not stock in the business) and usually pay some premium over the book value. The buyer expects to pay back the borrowed funds and put some profits in his pocket by making two basic improvements in the acquired business: lower operating costs and higher sales. There are huge pitfalls in both of these expectations.

Lower operating costs are very difficult to achieve (unless the acquired business is being "tucked in" to a strong existing operation with excess capacity). Many times the new owner actually ends up with *increased* operating costs. The new owner may feel the need to spend money in order to hang on to important customers and key people. Cutting costs can lead to loss of key people and important (that is, profitable) customers. The loss of profitable customers may lead to further cost cutting and, ultimately, a death spiral.

Higher sales are very difficult to achieve (unless the buyer is bringing something to the party, such as exclusive, hot product lines). In many cases, sales at the acquired company drop off the first year after the acquisition. The new owner may not be able to hold on to some accounts due to losses of key people and competitive reactions to the acquisition. The negative effects of cost cutting may result in falling sales, not increased sales.

Most acquisitive distributors don't purchase other distributors with the intention of reselling them at a big profit within a short period of time (such as five years). Such an investor might be willing to accept poor annual performance if he simply planned to quickly flip the businesses he bought. An example of this unusual approach is a consolidation play in which many small distributors are rolled up to create a large one. The investor is hoping for synergies of scale but also knows that large companies command higher prices than small ones. He expects to build the hypothetical billion-dollar, industry-dominant distributor and unload it at a handsome profit. That's not the same thing as building a top-quartile distributor brick by brick. Most acquisitive distributors cannot play the game at the level of the investment bankers, private-equity firms, or other big dealmakers.

Acquisitive distributors can, however, be swept up in the type of optimism that gets the big dogs into trouble. When paying a big premium (overpaying), the buyer has to be solid as a rock in his understanding of how he will repay the premium. The pathway to repaying that debt (whether a loan from the bank or just an obligation to the company's treasury) is not by hoping for expense reductions or increased sales.

Customer profitability analysis is the map to be followed.

CHAPTER ELEVEN

Customer Profitability Analysis

"Building deals on bedrock…"

Harvard Business Review, September 2004

• •

The acquisitive distributor is buying a set of customer relationships and the future stream of positive cash flow he expects to enjoy from transactions with those customers. In some cases, valuable supplier relationships are also an important part of the purchase. The transaction includes the people necessary to maintain and build on those relationships, and the inventory (and possibly facilities) needed to take care of those customers.

The buyer is taking a chance when paying a premium for these relationships and other assets. The future stream of positive cash flow is jeopardized if those fragile relationships (customers and suppliers) are imperiled in any way.

The buyer needs to know which customer relationships currently provide and will probably continue to generate positive cash flow in the future. The acquirer can then pinpoint the people (and suppliers) who sustain and nurture those profitable customer relationships.

The distribution of customer profitability is wider than thought

My book *More to the Bottom Line: Customer Profitability Tools for Distributors* (www.nawpubs.org) outlines a simple but powerful four-part method for distributors to

- Measure customer profitability.
- Rank customers by operating profit.
- Segment customers by profit potential.
- Focus the organization on customer profitability.

Much of the distributor's operating profit often comes from its relationships with a small number of highly profitable customers. And there is usually a handful of large customers whose transactions are not profitable for the distributor.

Customer profitability insights tell the acquisitive distributor what he needs to know: which customer relationships provide most of the operating profit. He can then identify which people (and possibly suppliers) are critical to the future of those crucial relationships. A sensitivity (risk) analysis of the high-profit customers will pinpoint external risks to the relationships.

Some examples of external customer risks, those outside of the acquirer's control, are

- Customers experiencing business problems including credit risks.
- Technology changes threatening the distributor's products.
- Prospective customer plant closings or production relocations.
- Personnel changes at customers.
- Upcoming expiration of major customer contracts.
- Competitive activities in the market and at specific customers.
- Customer relationships dependent on loyalty to the former owner.

Other risks outside the acquirer's control include the following people issues:

- Company staff close to retirement or with major health concerns.
- People working without commitments not to compete with the company (especially those with frequent job changes in their employment history or who have worked for competitors in the past).
- People who seem antagonistic to the ownership changes or who would otherwise be unhappy or unproductive due to poor cultural fit.
- Company staff whose compensation packages are unrealistically high (risk of departure if they are reduced) or low (risk of departure if they are not increased).

The risk of losing the support of mission-critical suppliers may be unavoidable in some distributor acquisitions. Customer profitability information will lead the buyer to suppliers whose continued support is needed for ongoing profitability. Some of the external risks include consolidation of supplier ownership, supplier management changes, antagonism toward the new owner, and loss of supplier loyalty that was based on the relationship with the former owner.

It is impossible to perform a sensitivity analysis on all customers, people, and suppliers during due diligence. Customer profitability information directs the acquisitive distributor to the customers, staff, and suppliers where risk analysis is *imperative*.

Buying profitable customers at a premium can be a good investment

Even though it may seem that acquirers buying customer relationships in bulk should receive a quantity discount, they actually often pay a premium. For the right acquisition, with the right kind of profitable and stable customer relationships, paying what appears to be a large premium may be a wise investment.

Customer profitability information can direct the acquirer toward opportunities to build the target company's operating profits. For example, some of the target company's largest customer relationships may cause operating losses. These relationships may be good candidates for win-win negotiations with customers to uncover the root causes of the losses (small orders, slow payments, and slow-moving custom inventories).

Customer profitability data may reveal company-wide profitability issues, such as a small-order problem, unrealistic prepaid freight policies, or sales compensation plans that encourage unprofitable orders. Rethinking the target company's sales policies can provide long-term profitability improvement for many of its customer relationships.

Other uses of customer profitability data include segmentation of customers based on profit potential and a disciplined approach to developing new services (value propositions) for high-profit customers.

These types of profitability improvement are not quick fixes. They represent the kind of long-term, patient investment approach needed to protect and enhance relationships with the most profitable customers.

I'm opposed to quick fixes generally, and especially to the idea of firing unprofitable customers. Many times, unprofitable relationships can be repaired to the benefit of both parties. Some customer relationships are money losers but have strategic value to the distributor, such as enabling access to an important product line or providing an entry point into a new market.

Some unprofitable customer relationships cannot be fixed and do not represent other value to the distributor. Raising prices and cutting back "free" services may result in the customer's firing himself (no damage caused) or he may realize that the distributor is valuable to him after all. If the customer takes his business elsewhere, the distributor will not benefit unless he has the resolve and ability to reassign resources to other customers, or reduce operating costs including unnecessary people costs.

Understand your own customer profitability

Customer-profitability information is not simply a tool for analyzing target companies in acquisitions. Top-quartile performers need to master the art and science of customer-profitability analysis if they intend to stay in the high-performance category. Other distributors need to become proficient if they aspire to reach the top quartile.

In *More to the Bottom Line* I argue that anything less than top-quartile profit performance is dangerous. Mediocre performers may not generate enough cash flow to finance their own growth. Most distributors that don't have some growth fuel start to wither. They can't attract and hold on to the people and suppliers they need to maintain the right customer relationships.

The acquisitive distributor must become proficient at measuring customer operating profit, ranking and segmenting customers, and focusing on customer profitability to manage the business. These well developed skills are critical to the mission of becoming a low-risk, serial acquirer of smaller distributors by making a small acquisition every year, or as fast as your company can get it done well.

Great companies/small acquisitions

Many great distributors have been built brick by brick without making Big-Bang acquisitions. Some formerly great distributors have sustained permanent damage by making one acquisition too many. To avoid offending anyone, I won't name any names. You know who some of them are.

Distribution has been described as a prosaic business. While we may appear dull to some observers, we can make good money. My idea of excitement does not include betting the equity and reputation of a well established and successful business on one (possibly foolish) idea. Those distributors who enjoy taking huge risks would be better off visiting Caesar's Palace. (At least the casino will give big spenders free drinks and tickets to a show.)

I recommend taking measured, affordable risks. The acquisitive distributor can supplement his slow-but-steady organic growth by making a series of small and digestible acquisitions. As mentioned elsewhere in this book, my definition of a small acquisition is the addition of about 5% to revenues while risking less than 10% of the company's equity. Digestibility varies with the complexity of the acquired company, including its culture, location, product and customer fit, and the compatibility of its people and systems.

Customer profitability information from the target company can help quantify the risks, identify profit improvement opportunities, and pinpoint the customers and people (and possibly suppliers) who must be protected at all costs.

Customer profitability information is indispensable to help assure the success of the due diligence and implementation phases of acquisition of a distributor.

High performance companies in our "prosaic" business manage to generate a sparkling return on investment without gobbling up mountains of capital.

Many distributors have done a masterful job in optimizing their profitability, even within the limitations of slow-growing sales volume. The top-quartile performers have tweaked their asset management, gross margin, and operating expense controls to squeeze superior operating profits out of lackluster sales. The most elite distributors have devised profitable new services for their customers—services that generate fees above the traditional gross margin earned on product sales.

Top-quartile distributors don't lack imagination, but many are challenged to grow their revenues at a satisfying rate. Sales volume is driven by demographics and industrial production for many traditional distribution product lines. Distributors doing business in a confined geographic space may find themselves chasing their tails when looking for opportunities to build sales. Slow population growth in many parts of the U.S. and the deterioration of the domestic manufacturing sector have compounded distribution growth challenges.

Marginal sales opportunities (going after someone else's ugly, unprofitable customers) are tempting when there is no sales wind at one's back. Putting the right spin on the numbers may persuade managers that unattractive new sales volume will somehow be profitable when added to their own company's base of profitable business. The unfortunate result may be unreasonable risk of loss of capital (receivables and custom inventories) and an increase in the company's breakeven point. The added volume often necessitates investment in added capacity that is hard to eliminate if and when a large chunk of business evaporates.

Distributors need an ongoing supply of attractive, new, profitable customers to provide the seed corn for the business. A steady growth rate attracts the employees and suppliers needed to thrive. The right employees and suppliers attract the customers the distributor needs to assure continued success. Customer profitability analysis reveals the attractive customers.

A series of carefully calculated, small acquisitions provides the ready source of profitable new customers needed to sustain an attractive, or even exciting, growth rate. The risk of smaller transactions going awry is lower than the bet-the-farm dangers of Big-Bang acquisitions. The problems caused by a small acquisition that turns out badly can often be fixed without too much pain. The damage in even the worst-case scenario of a failed small transaction will not be fatal.

Many distributors who could benefit from a series of small acquisitions are reluctant to buy companies. They have heard too many horror stories from other distributors. The factors that cause deals to go bad, most often failed due diligence and fumbled integration, can be managed to avoid the shoals. Professional advice is available at reasonable cost to maximize the chances of success. Acquisitive distributors can learn from the mistakes of others.

A distribution business that's chugging along with an average annual growth rate of 3% per year will double in size every 24 years. The same distributor who becomes acquisitive and makes a small (5% of sales) acquisition every year will grow at a compounded annual rate of 8%. That distributor will double in size every *nine* years.

APPENDIX

*Evergeen Consulting's
Distribution Industry
M&A Survey*

Public and private companies

Investment research firms publish a wealth of data about mergers and acquisitions of public companies. Most of the information is derived from required by the SEC. Regulated entities are forced to divulge many of the details of their acquisitions and divestitures. Many companies volunteer additional background to the press to promote their stock or for other public relations reasons.

Privately held companies are far more secretive. Many managers consider detailed information about M&A activity to be highly sensitive. Transactions where both the buyer and seller are private companies are usually off-limits to researchers.

The secrecy surrounding M&A between private companies creates a conundrum for anyone attempting to compile, analyze, and present transaction statistics. Owner-managers willing to provide information generally do so only selectively, and usually under a cloak of anonymity. Sketchy or anecdotal information cannot be used for meaningful comparisons, and there is usually not enough raw data available to do serious work.

Distributors

The wholesale distribution industry, made up predominantly of private companies, presents a serious challenge for collectors of M&A facts. There are transactions in which both buyer and seller are public companies, and sometimes good information is available about deals in which one or both of the two parties is a public firm. Firms such as MergerStat and CapitalIQ obtain and study M&A information and publish their material for use by financial professionals.

It's difficult for the acquisitive distributor to make sense of the valuation ratios and other statistics flowing from the very large transactions that public companies engage in. The multiples found in large transactions don't match up well with the numbers usually seen in deals between smaller companies.

Per one industry source, between 1995–2004, the peak years for larger transactions in the distribution category were 1999 and 2000 (1,120 and 1,130 transactions). The low point was 1995 (68 transactions). Following the peak years, activity dropped off to 920 in 2001 and 640 in 2002, picking up again in 2003 to 782 transactions. The reported activity in 2004 was 819 transactions.

The multiple of "total enterprise value" (TEV) to sales in larger deals, as reported by MergerStat, fluctuated widely among the various wholesale lines of trade as well as from year to year. For example, the TEV/Revenue multiple for 2004 was 1.47 and the range was from .40 (media) to 2.60 (electrical). From 1998-2004 the peak year was 2002 with a 3.25 average TEV/revenue multiple. The range was from .74 (media) to 12.14 (electrical). The non-durables multiple was 1.51 in 2004, very close to the durables multiple, 1.45. In other years, 2003 for example, the difference was great (durables .73, non-durables 1.07).

This leads to two conclusions:

- Even from the best sources, the most reliable information we can get is erratic and hard to understand.
- The data we have about large transactions are not comparable to the world of smaller transactions.

How can the acquisitive distributor get his hands on more useful information? And what information is most useful?

The four most useful data elements about a transaction are

1. Purchase price, including debt assumed.
2. Sales revenue for the most recent year.
3. Operating profit for the most recent year (see below).
4. Net worth (book value).

Financial analysts might say that EBITDA (earnings before interest expense, depreciation, and amortization) is preferable to operating profit. The idea of EBITDA is to understand how much cash flow the business generates toward repayment of its debt. I like to use operating profit for analyzing distributor transactions. It is a before-income tax and before-interest expense number, and depreciation (and amortization) isn't significant for most distributors.

Survey of trade association members

Our survey of member companies of industry trade associations about their M&A practices was designed to gather information about the following:

- M&A activity level, past 10 years and next five years.
- Three largest acquisitions: statistics, satisfaction.
- Most successful and least successful acquisitions; underlying causes.
- Use of outside advisors.
- Best practices/worst practices in the four deal-making phases:
- Acquisitions strategy.
- Deal negotiating and structure.
- Due diligence.
- Integration.

The Internet-based survey form went to CEOs of member companies of line-of-trade associations belonging to NAW. A total of 416 distribution executives responded to the survey.

Of the respondents, 292 identified their primary line-of-trade association. Of the 62 different associations named, the most frequently mentioned were

1. National Association of Electrical Distributors (32).
2. Independent Distributor Association (23).
3. International Sanitary Supply Association (17).
4. Material Handling Equipment Distributors Association (16).
5. American Supply Association (16).
6. Heating, Airconditioning & Refrigeration Distributors International (14).
7. Fluid Power Distributors Association, Inc (12).
8. Association for High Technology Distribution (10).
9. Association for Hose & Accessories Distribution (10).
10. Gases and Welding Distributors Association (8).

11. National Paper Trade Association Inc (8).

12. North American Building Material Distribution Association (8).

Exhibit A-1 breaks down the distribution revenues of the 401 respondents who identified their sales volume.

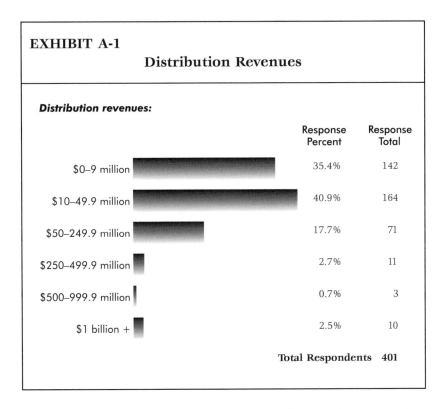

EXHIBIT A-1

Distribution Revenues

Distribution revenues:

	Response Percent	Response Total
$0–9 million	35.4%	142
$10–49.9 million	40.9%	164
$50–249.9 million	17.7%	71
$250–499.9 million	2.7%	11
$500–999.9 million	0.7%	3
$1 billion +	2.5%	10
	Total Respondents	**401**

With 76% of the companies below $50 million in sales, the typical acquisitions would necessarily be too small to compare directly with the deals made by the industry's largest companies.

403 indicated their number of locations, as shown in Exhibit A-2.

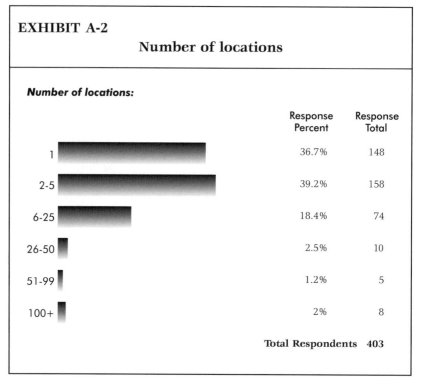

EXHIBIT A-2

Number of locations

Number of locations:

	Response Percent	Response Total
1	36.7%	148
2-5	39.2%	158
6-25	18.4%	74
26-50	2.5%	10
51-99	1.2%	5
100+	2%	8
	Total Respondents	**403**

Over three-quarters of the respondents are local or regional distributors with five or fewer locations.

Of the companies in the survey, 96% are under private ownership. Almost 90% of the survey respondents have the title CEO or President. Their role in their company's acquisitions follows in Exhibit A-3:

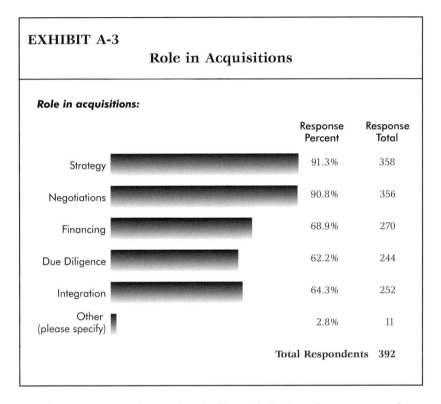

EXHIBIT A-3

Role in Acquisitions

Role in acquisitions:

	Response Percent	Response Total
Strategy	91.3%	358
Negotiations	90.8%	356
Financing	68.9%	270
Due Diligence	62.2%	244
Integration	64.3%	252
Other (please specify)	2.8%	11
Total Respondents		**392**

The 392 executives who indicated their role seem to place much more personal emphasis on the strategy and negotiations phases of their deal making, as opposed to the due diligence and integration phases.

Data elements for analyzing transactions

Survey respondents provided at least one data element (price, sales, operating profit, or book value) for 164 of their acquisitions. Price was stated for 159 deals, operating profit for 117, and book value for 92.

Price to operating profit

It is possible to derive a price to operating profit ratio for 93 of the reported transactions of profitable companies (that is, where both price and operating profit are stated, and the operating profit is positive). Based on an aggregate purchase price of approximately $523 million and an aggregate operating profit of approximately $85 million, the aggregate ratio 6.2, or the aggregate price is 6.2 times the aggregate earnings. The average price/operating ratio of the 93 transactions is 7.9.

Why the large difference? The 6.2 number is a weighted average of all of the deals, meaning the largest deals influence the total more than the smaller ones. The 7.9 figure gives equal importance or weight to each of the deals. Which is more useful? It depends. The data are from transactions in a variety of industries, over a number of years, and a range of deals both large and small. The deals database includes turnaround situations where the target company had been operating at a loss. Those transactions are left out of the above price/operating profit computations.

The range of ratios runs from .1 to 100, with a median value of 5.0. Half of the ratios derived from the values reported are between 3.3 and 8.0.

Price to book value

Both a price and a (positive) net book value were reported for 103 transactions. The aggregate price paid was $436 million and the aggregate net book value was $255 million. The price to book value ratio of the aggregate amounts is 1.71. The average value of the 99 transactions, giving equal weight to each deal, was 9.02, even after excluding four huge multiples that distort the result. The median of all the 103 ratios is 1.65 and the range of 50% of the deals runs from .38 to 10.0.

Price to sales revenue

Price and sales revenue were available for 156 transactions totaling $767 million in price and $1.9 billion in sales. The price/sales ratio for these aggregate numbers is 40.0%. The average of the derived ratios for the 156 transactions is 41.2%. The median is 33% and the range of 50% of the deals runs from 21% to 50%.

Making sense of the ratios

What do these data tell us? How can we turn them into useful information? First, let's remember that none of the figures can be verified. They are self-reported, through a survey. Second, recognize that people don't record or report numbers in the same way, even in the best of circumstances. For example, trailing profits may be for the most recent 12 months, for an average of the last two or three years, or a weighted average. The bottom line is that we are looking for broad guidelines, impressions, rather than for scientific precision.

So what have we learned? Take a group of transactions in which distributors purchased other distributors between 1994 and 2004. The total purchase price is over $750 million, of companies with sales of nearly $2 billion and operating profits are almost $85 million. The average sales were close to $12 million, with an average purchase price of just under $5 million. For the typical deal, the purchase price was about 40% of sales. The price was around 1.7 times book value. The price was between six and eight times operating earnings.

Breakdown by industry

Breaking the survey down into thin slices—such as by industry—poses two problems. First, the detailed information may risk exposing the sources of the information for those industries where knowledgeable insiders can speculate about who bought whom. Second, the number of transactions by industry is fairly small. The leading industries in the survey, by number of transactions, are (alphabetically):

- Building materials.
- Electrical.
- Gases and welding.
- Hydraulic equipment.
- Material handling.
- Paper.
- Pet supplies.
- Plumbing and HVAC.
- Sanitary supplies.

For the above nine industries, the price/sales ratios range from 21% to 85%, the price/operating profits ratios range from 2.4 to 18.7, and the price/book value ratio from .53 to 4.93. Each of the industries reported at least five transactions. The median values:

Price/operating profit	7.5
Price/book value	1.77
Price/sales	34.9%

Note that broad ranges are seen, even within a narrow band of transactions. The median values, which reduce the distortions of unusually high/low numbers, tend to cluster. This may be helpful as a yardstick, but the point is that no two companies are exactly alike. And the same buyer will pay different prices at different times depending on conditions in the market and issues facing the buyer's company. Buyers often pay more when there is competition for the seller. Some sellers are more skilled than others at preparing their companies for sale. Some buyers and sellers are better negotiators. Personal factors such as age or health enter into the equation. Some sellers and buyers get better advice than others. Lady luck plays a role. And timing is everything.

Buyer satisfaction with acquisitions

Magazine and newspaper articles often report that mergers and acquisitions don't work. That is fairly easy to calculate for large, public companies. Analysts put a pencil to the calculation of shareholder value added (or subtracted) as the result of an acquisition. This is trickier to do for transactions in which the buyer is a privately owned company. There is no easy way to determine shareholder value in the absence of quoted prices for the company's shares. So I decided to ask distributors how satisfied they were with their acquisitions. The key questions are "Did the acquisition meet your expectations?" and "Why or why not?"

Root causes of success and failure

The following exhibit plots the buyers' overall satisfaction with their purchases against three deal-making financial ratios: price paid related to the target company sales, target company earnings, and target company book value. Were buyers happier with transactions in which they got a great deal and less happy with deals where they stretched? Based on Exhibit A-4, there is no correlation between price and satisfaction. Perhaps buying companies is like buying automobiles: Why would you want to get a great deal on a car you don't want?

EXHIBIT A-4
Acquirer Overall Transaction Satisfaction

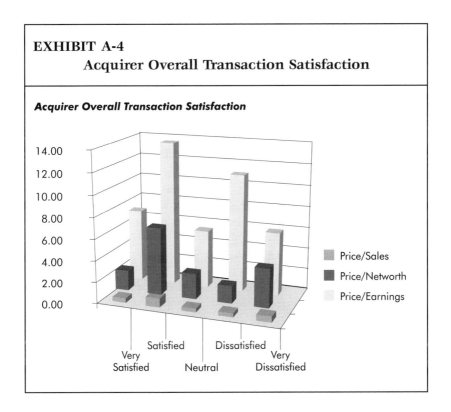

Acquirer Overall Transaction Satisfaction

The Exhibit A-5 plots the buyers' overall satisfaction with their deals against their functional effectiveness in the four deal making phases: strategy, negotiation, due diligence, and integration. Bingo! There is indeed a positive correlation between deal making skill and satisfaction with the outcome. The gap, or "delta," is particularly wide with integration (rating of 1.0 is highest, 5.0 is lowest):

Strategy	.33
Negotiation	.89
Due diligence	.82
Integration	1.10

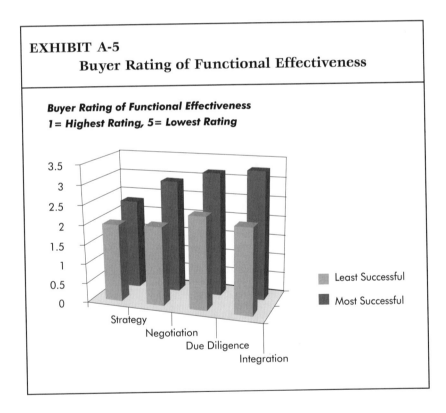

EXHIBIT A-5
Buyer Rating of Functional Effectiveness

Buyer Rating of Functional Effectiveness
1= Highest Rating, 5= Lowest Rating

Least Successful
Most Successful

The acquisitive distributors evaluated their acquisition strategies about the same for both their most and least successful deals. The difference was nearly three times as great for negotiation and due diligence, and the gap was close to four times as large for integration.

Recall that the CEOs spent much more of their time on the strategy and negotiation phases of their company's deals and much less on the due diligence and integration phases.

Personal interviews

As a follow-up to the survey, we interviewed 50 distribution executives with experience acquiring other distributors. The structured interviews were designed to

- Record first-hand stories about distributor acquisition experiences.
- Analyze the lessons learned from those experiences.
- Solicit advice for distributors about to make an acquisition.

We wanted to learn more about best and worst practices in distributor acquisitions, to give some life to the data, and to validate our findings. The executives were urged to tell us stories about their experiences, some of which are summarized and appear in the preceding chapters.